Rob Kemp is a freelance journalist and author of the best-selling book *The Expectant Dad's Survival Guide*. His work on the subjects of fatherhood and parenting features on the Boots Parenting and MSN websites and has appeared in a number of national newspapers and magazines, including the *Guardian*, the *Independent*, the *Mirror*, *Men's Health*, *FQ*, *Pregnancy*, *Baby and You*, *Pregnancy & Birth* and *Mother & Baby*.

THE NEW DAD'S SURVIVAL GUIDE

What to expect in the first year and beyond

ROB KEMP

Vermilion
LONDON

3 5 7 9 10 8 6 4

First published in 2014 by Vermilion, an imprint of Ebury Publishing
A Random House Group company

The Random House Group Limited Reg. No. 954009
Addresses for companies within the Random House Group can be
found at www.randomhouse.co.uk

Penguin Random House is committed to a sustainable future for
our business, our readers and our planet. This book is made from
Forest Stewardship Council® certified paper.

Printed and bound in Great Britain by Clays Ltd, St Ives plc

ISBN 9780091948115

To buy books by your favourite authors and register for offers visit
www.randomhouse.co.uk

The information in this book has been compiled by way of general
guidance in relation to the specific subjects addressed, but is not a
substitute and not to be relied on for medical, healthcare, pharmaceutical
or other professional advice on specific circumstances and in specific
locations. So far as the author is aware the information given is correct
and up to date as at June 2014. Practice, laws and regulations all
change, and the reader should obtain up to date professional advice on
any such issues. The author and publishers disclaim, as far as the law
allows, any liability arising directly or indirectly from the use, or
misuse, of the information contained in this book.

'They don't really do much at first'

(How some new fathers see some new babies ... and vice versa)

CONTENTS

INTRODUCTION
WE'VE ALL GOT TO START SOMEWHERE ...

When I wrote a book for expectant dads a few years back it was at a time when there wasn't much on the market for men who'd been in the same boat as me. I wasn't sure that there'd be a great demand among men for a book telling them what pregnancy was all about.

But I knew from my own experience, and from talking to new dads and those that were about to become parents for the first time, that something that could provide some useful insight, some practical tips and some hands-on guidance – along with a large dollop of 'what to expect' – would be a whole lot better than nothing at all.

Sure enough, the book was something men – and plenty of women – really did want, and they went out and bought it. More important was the feedback I got from those who read it. It highlighted the fact men *do* want to know what's happening with their partner when she's pregnant. They *do* want to know how that little baby is developing and what can help it grow to become a healthy little son or daughter. Men *do* want to know how to deal with the emotional stress, the physical strain and the financial headlock that can come during such a tense time. And why wouldn't we?

Through prenatal, pregnancy, post-partum and pretty much every day, fathers are more and more involved in the raising of their children these days. Changes in the way that both sexes work, new family-friendly laws and the attitudes of society have all helped re-shape the role of the modern father.

And it's crucial that we do become more actively involved from the start and remain hands-on as our children develop and find their way in the world.

Dads are different. The way we play with our kids, the influences we have, the bonds we form differ greatly from the way mums do things. And yet in recent times the role of the father in child development has been downgraded – often by fathers themselves – by those who subscribe to the school of thought that, while it's great to have dads around, they're not essential to raising rounded kids ready to face what the world throws at them.

Never ever underestimate your influence upon your child and your role as a father – especially in the first year of their life, when it can seem at times as if they're something from another planet and you've got little more than a walk-on part in the family set-up. The bonds you build at this time and the habits that form in this first stage of fatherhood can and will set the trend for the relationship you have with your child for years to come. Not only that but it will have a crucial influence upon how they interact with their own offspring too one day.

As a father the best advice I can give to new dads is to get 'stuck in' as soon as you possibly can. You will experience a multitude of mixed emotions along the way. Sometimes they can be feelings of indifference or reluctance about your role – other times your little baby will make you feel better than you've ever done before. Don't be alarmed if you find it tough to bond with this new, life-changing member of your family – but don't be afraid to do so either.

The bulk of the advice and guidance in this book comes from experts, medical specialists, baby development know-alls and most importantly from dads of all types who've been there before you. Much of the advice I've sought has been backed-up with the 'wisdom of fathers' – first-person testimony from dads who've 'been there', 'done it' and have a milk-stained T-shirt to prove it. They've picked up a few useful tips along the way and made plenty of mistakes that we can learn from.

Where possible I've looked to cover everything you can expect to happen in the first year or so as a new dad – in the format of questions that you may well find yourself asking as you get used to the role.

Each chapter covers a month of your child's life from birth and what's generally likely to be happening with them, with you and with your partner around this time. But, as you'll soon find out, no two babies are the same and everyone's experience of parenting is different. As a result you may find yourself dipping into chapters you hadn't planned on reading and going to places you really didn't expect to – that's pretty much how fatherhood will pan out from now on.

I've also included tips and insight into ways you can bond, communicate and play with your child now and as they go beyond year one and into the time of toddling.

The idea of the book is to provide a service for new dads. It's meant to arm you with some skills and know-how – but not to preach. Nor is it designed to provide an instruction manual on how to parent or the best way to bring up your baby (there will be plenty of people wanting to tell you how to do that unfortunately).

Dip in and out of this book at your leisure. (Ha! Leisure, remember that?) Glean whatever useful tips you can – and be sure to pass them on, because one thing I discovered during the writing of this book and the previous one is that dads don't talk enough about being dads. It's like 'Dad Club' obeys the first rule of Fight Club and no one talks about fatherhood.

It's a real shame because, as I'm sure you'll find out too, when dads do share information and pass on experiences it's usually really useful, practical, tried-and-tested advice. The kind of stuff that makes you feel more comfortable being a father and more confident in dealing with the challenges that modern fatherhood brings about. Some of which I'm hoping you'll discover in the pages that follow and make your own. Best of luck ... enjoy the ride.

1 DAWN OF THE DAD

Child's Life: Weeks 0–4

THE STATS

A few ballpark statistics that may apply to your little boy or girl right now:

Newborn baby: UK average weight is 3.4 kg (7½ lb). Enter your child's here:_____

On entering the world your baby can suddenly go on a crash diet. It's nothing to do with the demand for them to be photographed in public but simply a natural process that sees them poo and wee away about 10 per cent of their body weight. It can alarm a new mum especially – almost as much as the weird poo they do (called meconium) can startle a new dad – but rest assured that after about 10 days most babies are back at their fighting birth weight.

Average length from crown to toe: 50 cm (20 in). Enter your child's here:_____

Eyes: these are about 75 per cent of their adult size, but babies' vision is far from 20/20. Newborns can focus best at a distance of about 30 cm (12 in) away – within three months that should normalise.

5

Peeing: some babies can and will wee every 20 minutes.

Bones: 300 – that's 94 more than adults have. The bones fuse as they grow.

Birth marks: four out of five infants have some form of birthmark ... get searching!

HOW IT ALL BEGINS ...

It's a tricky one knowing where exactly to start this guide. The obvious answer is from the moment you physically become a father to a little boy or girl (or both) for the very first time.

I'm going to assume that you're not exactly thumbing through these pages while holding your partner's hand as she, in turn, asks the surgeon to perform a double knot on the umbilical cord. (You're keen to find out more about your role, I bet – but not *that* keen.)

So let's kick off at year zero as a new dad with a brief recap over what you've just been through. Apologies in advance if you read the predecessor to this book – *The Expectant Dad's Survival Guide* – and things seem a little familiar in places; there's a bit of an overlap when father-to-be meets dawn of the dad.

Now, cast your mind back to just over seven months ago. Just about the time you heard those magic words 'I'm pregnant' (and quite possibly thought of two words of your own in response). Since then you've both been through the most turbulent time emotionally, physically and quite possibly financially in the history of your relationship so far.

Your partner/girlfriend/wife/fiancée/shotgun bride will have been prodded, probed, scanned, rubbed, advised, measured, investigated, nagged, confused, weighed, injected, scanned again and weighed some more. She may well have suffered countless anxious moments, thrown up, leaked from places she wasn't expecting to, cried for no discernible reason, screamed for some very valid reasons and had at least half a dozen complete strangers reach out and touch her baby-storing stomach like it's the 'This is Anfield' sign at some time or another.

You'll have been there to witness this all – and what you haven't been there to see will still have been relayed back to you in gory detail. You too could well have been waiting nervously for the results of tests, experienced scares, felt the panic of false alarms and endured moments when you were powerless to do anything more than stand there in the new and unfamiliar position of being relied upon to provide comfort and support. You'll possibly have argued over names, probably had rows about baby accessories and almost definitely experienced a bust-up over family involvement. Thorny topics of conversation during the pregnancy may already have included 'helping out around the house', 'money', 'going out', 'staying in' – or the fact that 'all we do these days is argue'.

And then you'll also have shared moments when you see those first images of your child moving in the womb, or heard their heartbeat, or been given that first present for the baby, or felt those first movements or kicks, or discussed names, or designed the nursery or just dwelt upon how life is going to change forever for you both.

And all of that before the birth.

No matter what you read before or what classes you attended or whatever the advice you took it's unlikely that anything prepared you fully for the birth of your first child. How can it? That moment is uniquely special to every father – though some will still play it cool and refrain from admitting just how much it means to them.

Of course, that birth could have gone like clockwork for you all. It could have passed smoothly with barely a murmur from mother, baby, medical staff or concerned relatives. But that's highly unlikely.

That birth of your first child was a life-changing experience for all of you. Whether it was the rush to get back from wherever you were in time for the birth, or the trauma of complications, or the angst of waiting, or the struggle to find out what was happening, or the stern insistence from the midwife that you didn't keep ringing the help bell, or the unsuitable temperature in the birthing pool, or the battle to stick to the birth plan, or the sheer horror that struck when a word like 'complication' was mentioned, or the desperate cries for 'drugs' or just the out-and-out surreal process of having countless different people with name badges on their lapels gazing at your partner's privates while you were selecting a soothing 'music to have a baby by' track and fending off text message requests for updates from your sister-in-law – there's no way that birth is something you'll forget in a hurry.

So take a moment to take stock.

Ask yourself whether it was what you expected. For that matter, were you expecting a boy or a girl? If you didn't already know you may have got yourself into a mindset that right now will require some serious back-pedalling.

In the chaos that ensues, don't miss the chance for the pair of you, as new parents, to reflect on what's been an overwhelming nine months already.

When problems occur in relationships for new parents – and they commonly do – the cracks can often be traced back to the time around the birth. The words 'birth' and 'trauma' aren't linked by accident. And it's not just the mother and baby that can feel the impact. If you can, try to find the time to talk about the birth with your partner. When the dust has settled – and more crucially the scars are healing – tell her how it was for you; how you felt about her during the birth (honest, but positive!). Even discuss what you'd maybe do differently in future as an 'expectant dad'. By airing these thoughts now there's more chance that you will put any issues surrounding the birth experience to rest and that at least one of you will remember any of the great ideas you both come up with for the next time around.

Dad You Know?

Get a Grip

- A third of fathers don't know how to hold their baby for the first time.
- For 20 per cent of dads, the first baby they will ever hold is their own.
- It takes a fifth of dads one week on average to feel comfortable holding their little one, whereas many mums (62 per cent) feel it is a natural instinct from day one.

(Some stats from Persil Non-Bio)

HOW DO I HOLD MY BABY?

Life as a new dad is full of new experiences, sensations and purchases. One of the first tactile things you're going to do – possibly for the first time ever in your life – is to hold a newborn baby.

Get your hands nice and sticky pal, here's how it's done:

Forward pass

Unless you personally plucked your child directly from whence it appeared, the likelihood is it'll be handed to you by a member of the delivery team (NHS, not DHL). Now simply cradle both arms with your hands facing upwards – you've possibly seen Brazilian footballers do this as a goal celebration – overlapping at waist level. Let the baby's neck rest in the crook of one of your bent elbows. Use the rest of your 'cradled' arms to support the baby's body.

Cot's up, Doc?

If, however, you're picking your new baby up from a cot for the first time it's a whole different ball game. This time you slide one hand under the baby's neck – supporting the aforementioned neck in the palm of your hand, and their head with your fingers. When you do this the top of your baby's back will rest on your wrist. Now, here's the fun bit, slide the other hand under the baby's bottom. Either do this by slipping your hand between their legs or sliding it under the side of their bum so that it rests in the palm of your hand. When you're secure, gently lift them to your chest and then move your hand to put them in the cradle position. Try to hold your baby so that their head is slightly higher than their backside and always, **ALWAYS** support the head.

At first it can feel strange holding a baby, and you'll understandably be anxious with this precious, fragile little life in particular. But the more you do it, the more natural it becomes. There are people who've been paid research grants to confirm that this most basic of moves – man holds child – helps cement a lasting bond between father and baby for evermore.

Weird Things Babies Do

What's Up with my Baby's Head?

Even the most smitten new parent can find themselves sometimes looking at their wonderful new baby and asking themselves, 'What's going on with its head?' Don't shout it out but the truth is plenty of dads find their offspring a bit odd looking at times, especially around the cranial department. The reason for this is that a baby's head can take around 18 months to fuse together. Their skulls are made up of a series of plates that are squeezed together as they pass down the birth canal on their journey out of their mum's womb. Although some of the initial oddities on your baby's head – caused by birth implements like forceps or the ventouse cup – will heal up pretty quickly, other marks may take longer. A baby that has spent time in an incubator after their birth may develop a longer head that's flattened at the sides – this too will clear up in time as they're able to move their heads themselves and the bones correct themselves.

WHEN DO WE TAKE OUR BABY HOME?

Most babies are allowed home – accompanied by a responsible, ideally sober adult of course – within 24 hours of their birth. Some may have to be kept in for observation or special treatment. If your baby has been born premature (earlier than 37 weeks) or underweight; or needs extra help in breathing, feeding, generating body heat; or if they're suffering with any conditions affecting their heart or circulation, the hospital will provide special care for them until the all-clear is given.

When the midwife or specialist paediatrician who's been observing your baby is finally happy that all is well – and your partner feels up to leaving the creature comforts of the National Health Service – then they'll be discharged.

Don't hope for too much pageantry with your send-off. Most modern labour wards pretty much operate a 'hot bed' policy – no sooner will one new mother and baby be out through the turnstiles then another wailing woman with a swollen womb will be trundled in.

Basically you, your partner and your new son or daughter will find yourselves stood outside the hospital left to fend for yourself from now on ... The likelihood is they'll be looking at you, Dad, to come up with a carriage to get them home.

Wisdom of Fathers

Bringing Home the Baby

'When we walked out of the hospital we felt that we were going to get stopped at any time and asked to take our baby back, as we didn't feel that we were qualified!' Matt D

HOW DO I GET THEM HOME?

If you're driving them home from the hospital yourself you need to have a car seat for an 'age 0' child. This could be the car-seat-cum-carrier that comes with a travel system or a specific baby car seat (see Chapter 2 for more details). It'll save on time, swearing and embarrassment if you can get familiar with fitting this before your baby is ready to come home.

If you're taking your baby home by taxi then try to take the carrier along too. Some parents opt to hold their baby while travelling in the back of a cab or licensed taxi, but the driver may point out that the onus is on you – and not them – to make sure children are secure in the back of a taxi ... just in case you weren't anxious enough at this time.

Taking them home secured in a carrier as opposed to in your arms is a safer move. If it's a mini-cab firm, ask before booking them if they're able to take a child seat.

WHAT CAN MY BABY DO RIGHT NOW?

The old adage that babies 'don't really do much' is a harsh take on the fact that they're obviously in the early stages of the whole being-a-human thing. It's also a bit of a myth since your newborn will be able to do a bag of tricks including:

- **Blinking:** Their reflex actions are off and running and they'll shut their eyes to bright light. (Please don't reach for the torch, just take my word for it.)
- **Rooting:** Yes, yes, your baby is 'rooting' (no sniggering now, lads). This is the term used to describe another vital primitive reflex action, that of turning their head towards a stroke on their cheek. It's all part of nature's way of finding the breast – something some males never grow out of.
- **Sucking:** Babies have an incredibly powerful sucking facility, for reasons that really don't need a book to explain. Tease them with your little finger to see just how strong this action is, but don't keep doing it because if they don't get any milk it just pisses them off.

- **Swimming:** Babies can naturally swim in water – though they're limited to the front crawl for the moment. To be perfectly accurate it's called the 'dive reflex' or 'brady-cardic response' and causes babies to instinctively hold their breath and open their eyes when submerged.
- **Grasping:** Put your finger in the palm of your baby's hand and they'll close their fingers around it to grip you. The reasoning behind this 'palmer grasp' reflex may stem from a primitive 'grip' move – a security measure – linked to when our ancestors' babies were carried from tree-top to tree-top.
- **Stepping:** This one's a bit contrived to be honest. If you hold a baby upright they'll move their feet in walking-like movements. It doesn't mean they'll start walking properly any speedier if you force them to do this every day – in fact, much like the sucking thing you'll probably just annoy the nappy off them again if you keep doing it.
- **Yawning:** Want to make your baby open up its mouth? Try holding the palms of both its hands at the same time. It may trigger what's called the 'Babkin' reflex, which makes them open wide and yawn. No one knows why, but it's quite good fun to try it on them.

WHAT WILL THAT FIRST NIGHT AT HOME WITH OUR BABY BE LIKE?

Some dads play that 'first night' very cool – possibly because they're knackered anyway – and instead spend most of the night trying to put the new mum's mind at rest.

Others will be sat bolt upright all night, listening to every sound they imagine their baby is making – they don't make much noise at first. Watching the little one's every move – though there aren't many of those at this stage to be honest. Wondering if they're okay – the baby almost definitely is, it's the parents that are in need of zoning out.

FEEDING

HOW CAN I HELP WITH FEEDING?

Research shows that new mums are more likely to choose to breastfeed if they're sure their partner is positive about it – and it has been shown to have huge health benefits for both vendor and consumer in the long term.

She's much more likely to have a good experience if her partner supports her decision – which in turn will make your life a bit easier too. Aside from being the most natural method of giving your baby a decent dose of milk – along with immunity boosting antibodies and essential growth nutrients – breastfeeding is also very cheap and relatively simple compared to the alternative. But that doesn't mean it's in any way as easy as it looks – and that's where you come in. New mums often experience problems getting their baby to 'latch on' to their breast to start feeding. As your partner gets used to the feeding it's useful to know that:

- Some feeding sessions can last an hour or more at a time – especially in the early days – and any novelty will soon wear off. It's boring for her, and your company during feeding will be welcome.
- It helps them both if you encourage and comfort your partner as she perseveres with the breastfeeding. It can be excruciatingly painful at times and very taxing – your emotional and logistical support will be crucial to how she finds the experience in the early days.
- You may be needed to change the nappy before she starts feeding – or to fetch a pillow or nip to the kitchen to fetch drinks or snacks. In short don't see it as an excuse to nip out for a while unless you have permission.
- You can literally lend a hand to help your partner get your baby to latch on to her breast – especially useful if your partner has had twins.

─────── *Dad You Know?* ───────

Breast Figures

In the past five years the proportion of babies breastfed from birth in the UK rose by 5 per cent, from 76 per cent to 81 per cent. But Department of Health studies show that a fifth of mothers who start breastfeeding stop within the first two weeks. Another 36 per cent switch from breast to bottle within the next six weeks. At three months, the number of mothers breastfeeding exclusively is 17 per cent and at four months, 12 per cent. Exclusive breastfeeding at six months remains at around 1 per cent.

What if she doesn't want to breastfeed?

There are plenty of sound reasons why breastfeeding is considered the best, and most mothers will give it their all – but for some mothers it's certainly not as straightforward as simply whipping out a boob and applying one baby. You should prepare yourself for some frantic moments and sheer frustration as your partner attempts to get to grips with it.

Being female, having swollen breasts and combining them with the mouth of a hungry nipper is still no guarantee of success – and, even when it is, not everything will go to plan:

- Some mums struggle to get a good latch, causing poor feeding and weight gain.
- Some mums suffer from sore or cracked nipples.
- Some mums and dads have difficulty dealing with breastfeeding in public – it'll help to discuss what you're both feeling and even devise a plan of action that may mean you providing cover or just being on hand with the breastfeeding accessories.

Talk it through with your partner before and during her time feeding your baby – and try to keep things clear as to what you're both expecting to happen. Some mums may stop breast-feeding because of pressure or perceived pressure from their partner to do so. But the bulk of the medical research seems to show that for your baby's sake it's important that dads encourage their partner to breastfeed whenever they possibly can.

How can I help when she's breastfeeding away from home?

Some new dads can't wait for the moment to arrive when their partner switches from breast to bottle for good. They admit to feeling jealous that this newcomer is monopolising their partner's mammaries or else the embarrassment they feel when their partner whips out a breast in public to meet the demands of a ravenous nipper is too much to handle.

Consider the fact that your partner won't be feeling too cocksure about this either. As natural as it is, no woman – even the most liberated of feminists or glamour models – will feel 100 per cent at ease trying to do as Mother Nature intended in a corner of the coffee shop on a busy Saturday morning. What she'll most likely appreciate is her partner – you, the new father – stepping in and helping her out. Try:

- Getting a little closer to her and shielding her if she wants you to instead of feigning a sudden interest in Fairtrade coffee posters.
- Grabbing one of those muslin cloths you've been mystified by since you bought them to help protect her privacy or to wipe up any mess if she wants it.
- Not getting too concerned about the reactions of others. Instead dwell on the fact that US research shows how the odours given off by breastfeeding have been shown to heighten sexual desire in childless women. This is totally pointless information, I know – but it takes your mind off the whingers who think breastfeeding in public 'shouldn't be allowed'.

HOW CAN I TAKE OVER THE FEEDS?

When she is successfully churning the stuff out at almost industrial production rates then you may be able to help out by feeding your baby yourself. Breastfed babies feed pretty frequently – every two to three hours. Empathetic fathers (yes, mate, that's you) will familiarise themselves with the feeding routine and the breastfeeding armoury. Learn to:

- **Take over feeds:** If your partner is expressing breast milk into bottles – via a pump into a bottle (e.g. AVENT ISIS pump and bottle, £22.49 – you can take over feeds and allow your partner to rest or just do something else for a change.
- **Know how to prepare formula feed:** That's the powdered stuff used in place of breast milk.
- **Be up to speed with 'breast-cessories':** Are you able to identify, fetch and if need be shop for nipple shields? They're like mini Mexican hats used by breastfeeding mums to help their baby latch on or combat soreness. Okay ... and what about nipple pads? These are used to soak up any leaks.

Weird Things Babies Do

White Noise

Some babies with colic find the kind of 'white noise' created by a mis-tuned radio, a fan or a hairdryer strangely soothing. Try plugging one in and giving it a try next time they cry.

How do I help with formula feeds?

- **Follow the formula:** You'll find the serving suggestions on the label. This will tell you how much to use according to your baby's age. Don't feel the urge to 'add a spoonful for luck', stick to the recommended amount.

- **Test the temperature!** Before you start, drip a little milk on to your wrist to check that it's not too hot.
- **Warm it up:** Breastfed babies will be used to warm milk so, if you're taking stored milk from the fridge, sit it in a jug of hot water to warm it up a little.
- **Get comfy:** Take up a position that you can hold for at least the next 30 minutes (check that the TV remote is nearby) with your baby cradled in your arm and its head on your shoulder, and make sure there are plenty of muslins and bibs to hand.
- **Fill the teat:** Tilt the bottle so that the teat is kept full of milk.
- **Do the bottling up:** Don't just leave the empties around the house. Fill the steriliser and ensure there are clean bottles at all times. Get into the routine of cleaning and sterilising bottles. Is that bottle freshly sterilised? Teats too?

If it's the chemical type of steriliser that you are using, then you use the sterilising tablets or liquids – aim to have these done beforehand since the bottles and teats need time to soak and be rinsed out. The steam ones work like a kettle – cleansing the bottles in up to 15 minutes depending on how many you're sterilising. Let the bottles cool before using them. Microwave ones are easiest and take around six to eight minutes to steam clean the bottles.

HOW DO I BRING UP MY BABY'S WIND?

By learning how to gently burp your baby you reduce the trapped air in your baby's stomach – preventing them from bloating and from throwing up. Put a cloth over your shoulder and hold them against your chest, supporting their head and rubbing their back until they burp.

─── *Wisdom of Fathers* ───

Dads on Breasts

'We spent quite a bit of money on gear to help with expressing milk – it was worth it because I could get more involved and Clare could rest up a bit more, but it's not always easy to do, no matter how often she does it.' Allan, father of Taylor

'I spoke with my brother about his wife's breastfeeding before our baby arrived and he gave me good advice about helping to shield her when out in public and trying to keep things as normal as possible so that she can relax and the baby can get a proper feed. It's natural and so long as you remember that you can deal with any embarrassment.' Mark, father of Annabel

'If your partner is expressing milk don't forget to date-label the bottles before you put them in the fridge.' Dan, father of Alfie

WHAT CAN I DO TO BOND WITH MY NEWBORN BABY?

When mums breastfeed their babies it triggers the release of a bonding hormone called oxytocin which helps relax the pair of them – baby and mother – and so helps tie the knot of love and stuff between them.

Sadly, try as you might, Dad holding a bottle doesn't quite have the same chemical reaction, but that doesn't mean you can't start bonding too.

Talk to your feeding youngster – especially if you've already been using your voice to bond before the baby was born by talking to it when it was still in the womb. Watch how your baby reacts – see if you can be the first out of you and your partner to raise a smile or a giggle from them. If they frown or turn bright red in the face, they're probably pooing (see overleaf).

NAPPIES

HOW DO I KNOW WHEN THE NAPPY NEEDS CHANGING?

In the first 48 hours of your baby's life your partner's breasts produce a much stronger solution altogether – a substance called colostrum. This 'full cream' of the breast milk range is revered for its laxative effect – it'll bring on your kid's first poo.

That first baby poo will be nine months' worth of backed-up waste (okay, not technically accurate but it may whiff like it is). It's such a hot potato that it has its own name – meconium. It's often black, sticky and could be mistaken for coffee grinds – though you wouldn't want this in the base of your new 'You're the Daddy' mug.

For some new parents the baby's toilet habits become a topic of daily conversation. Whoever said that 'babies don't really do much' obviously hadn't seen the contents of a newborn's nappy. Your conversations will run a little along the lines of 'he's done a real stinker this morning!' Banter about who drew the short straw with nappy changes will replace previous relationship hot topics. It'll become Sod's Law that the moment you're all finally ready to leave the house, you'll detect a whiff of a 'fresh delivery'. And if you're ever struggling for a poo-related theme then the changing shade and nasal 'tones' you get from your baby's poo could be one to, er, chew over. These include:

- Loose orange/yellow inoffensive ones which are more common in breastfed babies.
- Eye-burning, solid brown ones, often deposited by babies drinking formula milk.
- Occasionally, when a baby is changing from breast to bottle, its poo can take on a green hue, though this can also occur in babies suffering with colic.

Weird Things Babies Do

Food Processing

A breastfed baby will mush food to faeces in around 15 hours – this can be double the time it takes bottle-fed babies.

Should I change them if they've only done a wee?

Removing a baby's nappy can trigger the exact opposite effect to what you want – the change in air temperature around their bladder can trip their personal sprinkler system and give you a soaking. But on the whole babies will, of course, go for a wee whenever they want – such disciplines as toilet training are a good year and a half away right now.

There's no rule as to how often your baby will poo or wee, but if they go for several days without a bowel movement, or if they're suffering with diarrhoea or peeing profusely, then you need to talk to your baby's GP or the health visitor.

Baby wee – just like the grown-up vintage – does contain ammonia and as such can irritate the skin, sometimes leading to nappy rash. In general dry, cool skin is least likely to trigger nappy rashes so:

- Change the baby whenever they've soiled their nappy.
- Clean them with warm water or baby wipes.
- Dry them gently and thoroughly with a soft clean towel and let them stay nappy-free whenever it's warm enough – and safe enough for your home furnishings to do so.

How do I actually change a nappy?

Never quite the stroll in the park that you'd think it is – especially when you've only ever done it before on a doll at an antenatal class – nappy changing is a skill the modern dad can soon master, so long as he abides by the golden rules:

- **Preparation:** Lay out the tools for the job beforehand: that's fresh nappy, wipes, disposal bag and cream.
- **Location:** Change nappies on the floor whenever possible – ideally on a plastic changing mat – you'll find it easier to grab stuff and your baby is highly unlikely to fall off.
- **Disposal:** Set the dirty nappy to one side for either binning or sterilising depending on the type you're using.
- **Application:** Be sure to apply the barrier cream you're using after you've cleaned up your baby before fitting the new nappy.
- **Sanitation:** Wash your hands after every change – you may feel the need to do this more than once when you take a sniff of your hands too. Washing your hands before a change may help too, especially if you've got greasy fingers – grease can cause adhesive tape on nappies to lose its stickiness.

What do I do about cleaning his 'privates'?

Most of what new mums know they either have an instinctive grasp for, or else they pick it up as they go. However, a mystery for many a new mother (and so a handy chance for you to step in with some Dad know-how) is what to do when it comes to baby boys and cleaning their baby boy bits. If you have a newborn son explain to her that:

His winkle needs to be pointing downwards before the nappy is closed to stop him peeing upwards and leaking out of his nappy.

It's okay to clean a boy's foreskin – in fact it's recommended – but not to retract it; just clean it as you would any other house or garden baby genitalia.

And cleaning up girls?

Okay dads, now here comes a new experience. Cleaning your little girl's privates. During her nappy changes you should use water-moistened cotton wool to wipe the area from front to back. (Wipe away from your baby's vagina and urethra – the opening through which she does a wee.) Wiping from front to back will help to prevent bacteria transferring from your baby's bottom to her vagina or urethra and causing an infection.

WHAT'S THE BEST WAY TO BATH OUR BABY?

And for when the nappy situation is dire, there's always the bath ... It's as crucial to father–baby bonding as a golf and drinking weekend in Spain is to football team bonding – and often equally as messy. Dads who bath their baby experience a relaxing hormonal surge – apparently. Certainly, some research from the University College London suggests that children were more likely to get into trouble in later life if they didn't have 'quality' time like baths from Dad when they were little 'uns. So here goes:

- Use a bowl of warm water at first, a baby bath support or a purpose-built baby bath ... which is essentially a bowl with added marketing.
- Put cold water in the bath first, then hot. This simple tactic should stop you running the risk of accidentally scalding your baby. If you're using the family bath for your baby cover the taps and if you have separate hot and cold taps you could fit a mixing valve to the hot one that will control the water temperature.
- Check the water isn't too hot. Make sure the bath water is warm but not hot before putting your baby in. (Water that's warmed to about 37°C (99°F) is just right – check out the Philips AVENT Bath and Room Thermometer (£16.99), which floats in the bath and tells you the temperature.
- Never put your baby into a bath when the water is still running. The water temperature can change quickly. And NEVER leave them alone in the bath for a moment.

- Have all the gear – cloths, baby shampoo, towel, rubber ducky, etc. within arm's reach.
- Support them with one hand and gently swish the water over them with the other. (You should not underestimate how slippery a wet little baby is.) If you're using soap avoid putting it on your baby's face.
- Make funny faces and noises to relax your child (hopefully). Even though they spent nine months paddling in an amniotic sac they still find baths a bit bemusing on the whole.
- Dab them dry with a towel. Although the bath may be warm, your baby can quickly lose heat when you take them out – so keep the room warm. When you lift your baby out of the bath, wrap them in a hooded towel and make sure they're fully dry before putting their fresh nappy on.
- Apply whatever lotions and potions you may be using to keep your baby's skin soft and smooth. Then dress them just in time for them to poo or spew again.

WHAT'S THE HEALTH VISITOR HERE FOR?

Okay, when I said you're left to your own devices I did omit to mention the health visitor. Where the local authority budget allows, they're provided to check on your baby's health and development and to ensure you're coping well with the new role. It's all part of an NHS child surveillance programme – it involves check-ups for your baby up until they're school age.

The number of visits they make will depend on the wellbeing of your baby – assessments also take place at the local clinic. The health visitor will usually contact you to tell you when they're due but they usually do check-ups at around 6 to 8 weeks, then 6 months, 9 months, 12 months and 24 months. But don't wait for their call if you have any concerns about your baby's health or development.

HOW DO I CONTROL THE CROWD OF WELL-WISHERS?

Another key role for Dad during those first few weeks after the birth is to manage Baby's social diary. That's right, despite being all new and wrinkly and odd smelling your nipper will be in great demand. 'It's great that people want to come and see your new baby but it's still a fragile time for you both,' explains Denise Knowles, new family advisor with Relate. 'Do take up the offers of help and don't miss the opportunity to share your new baby with their new extended family, but be sure not to overstretch yourself.' To keep a check on the flocks of visitors:

- Discuss with your partner how to control the demands of friends and family who want to come and see the baby. Remember that she is probably recovering from a difficult labour or possibly even a C-section and may have very little energy to make polite conversation with her brother-in-law while breastfeeding in front of him and fighting baby blues.
- Agree cut-off times and when people phone ahead, ask that they don't stay beyond a certain time. 'Never be afraid to say you're tired or you want to put the baby down for a sleep,' says Knowles. The priorities are your partner and your baby right now and no one will really be offended.
- Meet online. Use video phone services like Skype to present your baby to those living far away. Those first few weeks are manic and, for friends and family living overseas especially, video calls enable them to see you and your baby, say 'hi' and put off the visit until further down the line,' suggests Knowles.
- Bear in mind the reactions of any siblings and ensure they're not left feeling neglected when friends and family visit.
- Re-set your answerphone for the first week or so with a short summary for callers about the baby, birth and health

of the mother and then call folk back when you're both up to it.

- Give visitors the library treatment and ask them to put their phones on silent if you've done that with your own during your baby's nap times.
- Create an 'exit code' that you and your partner share and use it to initiate and evacuate any well-meaning but over-staying guests.

Wisdom of Fathers

Visiting Rights?

'Do NOT invite anyone round to see the baby for at least a week. Your partner either gets paranoid about exposing the baby to germs or feels uncomfortable because the house is a tip and she looks like crap. Also it's too stimulating for the baby – so they scream either during or after and then won't settle. If there's anyone you really want to see – go and visit them or meet people for a stroll in the park with the baby in the pram.' Paul S.

WHY ARE HER HORMONES STILL MAKING MISCHIEF?

You may have experienced a side effect of your partner's fluctuating hormones during her pregnancy. (You'll remember if you did.) The fun doesn't end for them the moment your baby is born either.

Some new mums will be hormonally all over the place for months after the birth. Be prepared for tears at the drop of a nappy as her oestrogen and progesterone levels head towards the relegation zone. The stress of a new baby and its effects on sleep, energy and self-esteem aren't helped by her body going through a repair process following nine months of traumatic change.

Emotionally it'll strain her enormously, and physically she could be experiencing drenching night sweats, phantom kicks as her uterus re-adjusts, clumps of her hair falling out, bleeding gums and wobbly teeth – not helped by all her calcium being hoovered up by your baby – heavier and irregular periods, vaginal dryness, milk leaking from her boobs, wee leaking from her – well you know where – plus aching breasts and inflamed feet and hands that trigger restless aches at night or cause pins and needles the moment she sits down.

In short she won't be responding to the name 'Happy bunny' right now.

While most new mums struggle but get through to the other side okay – ideally thanks to some support from us new dads – for a number of women these post-partum hormonal surges can add to or influence feelings of despair and depression. Be sure to familiarise yourself with the signs and possible actions a new dad can follow in the event of your partner experiencing postnatal depression (see Chapter 4 for more information).

PATERNITY LEAVE

AM I ENTITLED TO PATERNITY LEAVE?

Since 2003, men with the paternal responsibility to look after a new baby have had the right to take two weeks of paternity leave. In recent years the rules regarding paternity leave have changed with the introduction of additional paternity leave and greater flexibility for parents to share time off work during their baby's first year.

To qualify to take up to two weeks off work as 'paid' paternity leave, you must be:

- The biological father, or
- The mother's husband/partner (including same-sex relationships), or
- The child's adopter, or
- The husband or partner (including same-sex relationships) of the child's adopter, and
- An employee must have worked for the firm since before the pregnancy began. (You must still be employed when the baby is born to qualify for the paternity pay.)

WHAT PATERNITY PAY DO I GET?

Ordinary Statutory Paternity Pay (OSPP) won't have you popping the champagne corks – certainly don't expect to be awarded with an oversized Pools winner's cheque. At the time of writing it's worth £135.45 per week or 90 per cent of your average weekly earnings if that's less. It is paid to you by your employer who will deduct tax and National Insurance contributions before handing it over. Some employers top up this payment – though they only get refunded the OSPP amount by HM Revenue and Customs.

Because of the relatively poor amount of money paid, and in spite of recent changes and political promises to try to mirror more beneficial European systems, many working dads instead just opt for taking some of their annual leave around the time the baby is born so as not to lose out.

A diluted or piss-poor (depending on your viewpoint) version of the Swedish model of 'daddy months' has recently been adopted here – see Additional Statutory Paternity Pay below – but is only available to certain dads in certain situations and again the take-up is minimal.

Dad You Know?

Taking Leave

A YouGov survey (Work–life Balance: Working for Fathers? – Working Families 2010) found that 55 per cent of fathers take their full paternity leave. Of those who didn't, 88 per cent would have liked to but could not afford it while 49 per cent felt that they were too busy or their employer would not look favourably upon it.

What is Additional Statutory Paternity Pay (ASPP)?

From April 2011, fathers who are entitled to OSPP have also been entitled to Additional Statutory Paternity Pay (ASPP) – though there's a hefty lump of small print attached to this. A father must have earnings on average of at least the lower earnings limit for National Insurance during the eight weeks ending with the 15th week before the baby is due. ASPP is offered to dads as an enticement to care for a child under one – if the mother has returned to work before taking her full 52 weeks' maternity leave (whether she is employed or self-employed).

As the name suggests this is *additional* to the two weeks ordinary paternity leave – and you'll be entitled to receive ASPP as long as the mother has not exhausted her right to Statutory Maternity Pay (SMP) or Maternity Allowance (MA) when she returns to work. You should know:

- It has to be taken in multiples of complete weeks and as one continuous period.
- It can be started by the father at any point after the baby is 20 weeks old, and must be completed by the baby's first birthday.
- It is only available to working fathers who self-certify – providing a signed notification to his employer. (You can get one via HMRC.)

- All working terms and conditions of the father's employment contract will continue during ASPP time – with the exception of wages or salary.
- Both statutory and contractual holiday will continue to accrue.
- ASPP is paid at the lesser of the standard SMP rate (currently £135.45 a week) or 90 per cent of the father's average earnings – it's only payable during the period when the mother would have been entitled to SMP or MA. This means that a father can only claim ASPP between 20 and 39 weeks after the child is born.
- ASPP will be paid for a maximum of 19 weeks (though dads are entitled to take up to 26 additional paternity leave weeks) at the flat rate or 90 per cent of the father's average earnings, whichever is the lower figure.

So, as you see, it's not exactly tempting, is it?

The upshot of the low rate and jump-through-hoops process is that just 1 in 172 fathers is making use of it according to a study by the TUC in 2013 (only 0.6 per cent of the 285,000 dads eligible to take additional paternity leave did so).

HOW DO I KEEP UP WITH THE CHANGES IN PATERNITY PAY?

Much like a lot of what's going on around your baby right now, the situation with paternity and parental leave (time off after the baby is one year old) is somewhat fluid.

To keep up to date, or just to drive yourself around the twist perhaps, log on to www.gov.uk/parental-leave for the latest diktats or www.workingfamilies.org.uk – though here are some reported changes that will affect new dads soon:

Flexible working

The right to request flexible working is set to be extended to all employees who have worked for their employer for at least 26 weeks or more. (Due to come into law around April 2014.)

Flexible parental leave

Changes to introduce 'flexible parental leave' will not be 'live' until 2015, though proposals are to keep maternity leave and pay as it is now – with all women entitled to 52 weeks of leave and, if they qualify for SMP or MA, to 39 weeks of pay. Paternity leave will remain at two weeks, paid at the flat rate.

But if the family choose to share the mother's leave and pay they may do so – as soon as the compulsory maternity period has ended. A couple will have to self-certify to their respective employers their entitlement to leave and pay. (Both parents will need to qualify for leave and pay rights.)

A mother will end her maternity leave (or commit to ending it at a future date) to 'trigger' the family's move on to flexible parental leave. Couples will be able to share the remaining leave and pay as they wish – including taking the leave together – and each inform their employer of the amount of leave each wants to take, and the pattern of leave.

The maximum amount of pay will remain at 39 weeks and the leave will have to be taken at least by the time the child is one year old. Leave will be taken in weekly blocks, and the pattern – but not the amount of leave – may be vetoed by the employer.

Flexible parental pay for working parents who do not meet all the qualifying criteria for statutory payments may be introduced from 2018.

WHEN DO I TELL THE BOSS I'M TAKING TIME OFF?

In the event that you're reading this book well in advance of your baby arriving then it'll be useful to know that your employer will need – by law at least – a set period of notice about your intention to down tools and change nappies for two weeks after it's born.

Inform your boss/HR dept by the end of the 14th week before the baby's EDD (estimated due date).

WHAT HAPPENS WHEN I RETURN TO WORK?

Some new fathers may be counting down the hours to get back to work if they've taken leave to help out. Some fathers don't or can't take the time out anyway. Others will have some serious concerns about the health and well-being of their partner and baby when they do go back.

Most of us muddle through knowing that we're doing our bit by going out and bringing home the bacon – but at first it can be a genuine strain on the heart-strings for you. Your partner will have gotten used to having you there and will be anxious about how she will cope too. A few suggestions to make the return smoother are:

- **Have regular contact:** She's at home with a newborn baby while you're at work with a horde of overgrown babies. Set times when your baby won't be napping to call your partner and catch up – have stuff to tell her and ask her about how she's feeling as well as how the baby has been.
- **Talk away from the desk:** If you can, talk to her outside the workplace from your mobile phone or from a private room and ask to talk to your baby too. Don't rush this call either – remember that for her it could be the only decent chat of the day.
- **Take a picture:** Have a snapshot of your new baby to show workmates or make your baby pic your background image if you're working at a computer. It helps with building that 'bond'.
- **Keep it flexible:** If you're able to take advantage of flexible working practices – perhaps ones that mean you start earlier or finish later – try to work out with your partner what is the best balance. It could be influenced by the way

your baby is feeding or sleeping. Alternatively, compressing your working week so you can do four days at first could take some of the strain off all your family. If you want to look seriously into working more flexibly see Chapter 10 for more information about how you could go about this.

Put family first

Fatherhood provokes many working men to re-assess the way they work. Some will look to improve their status, role and pay packet in order to deal with their new responsibilities better. Others may seek out a whole new career or even change their work structure so that they're at home more. Whatever you do, for the first few months at least, try to identify the non-essential work-related activities that you may be able to eliminate from your weekly schedule for a while so that you are less stressed and are more likely to be able to leave on time.

Wisdom of Fathers

Life Changing

'We were really looking forward to Jemima being part of our lives, and were very aware of the effect it would have. It's been a really positive effect, and we were keen for Jemima to fit into our lives, rather than us changing ours drastically. I think some people assume that you're automatically going to become boring or change your life completely, but I'm certainly not. People seem surprised when they see how much we take Jemima out, and fit her into our life. That may prove more difficult as she gets a little older, but we'll see.' Michael, father of Jemima at four weeks old

Dad You Know?

Short Nights

Just 4 hours and 20 minutes – that's how much sleep new parents get a night on average, according to a poll of 3,000 new mums and dads. (Morrisons)

TOOLS OF FATHERHOOD

Child's Life: Weeks 5–8

WHAT'S HAPPENING WITH OUR BABY AT THIS STAGE?

From around the one to two months' mark, Daddy's little boy or girl may be doing some of the following stuff:

- Be awake for about 8–10 hours a day on average.
- Watching and following objects with their eyes.
- Holding their head up for short times.
- Smiling and laughing (remember them?).

Interacting with your baby continues to get more interesting as they become more responsive to you. Your voice is recognisable to them at this age – they're able to differentiate it from others as being a voice they know. Babies will start to smile from four to six weeks onwards – by this point you'll pretty much get a smile whenever they see you.

WHAT'S THE OBSESSION WITH OUR BABY'S WEIGHT?

The fixation with how much your baby weighs and their growth points on the scale of percentiles can come over as being a bit strong to the uninitiated (well, new) father. But at this stage the baby's weight-to-height (more length really since they don't stand up yet) ratio is one of the best indicators that they're growing healthily, that they're getting enough food and that you don't need to make any major changes to their diet. New mums, health visitors and the GP won't miss an opportunity to weigh the baby. Get used to helping out – maybe run a sweepstake on where they'll be at by three months to make all this effort worthwhile?

Weird Things Babies Do

See You, Daddy!

Your baby's vision and focus will sharpen and they'll follow around whatever interests them with their eyes. By around six weeks old they can follow a brightly coloured toy – ideally if it's held in their range of about 20 cm (8 in) away from them.

HOW WILL FATHERHOOD AFFECT MY FINANCES?

For many new dads, the last few months before the birth of their first baby may well have been spent wandering up and down the aisles of the maternity section of department stores, or else you'll have found yourself measuring car seats, test-driving pushchairs or swearing at flat-pack cots.

However, time constraints, finances or the whole struggle of coming to terms with the fact that you're going to become a dad may mean that you've not actually bought much of the stuff you'll need to keep your baby safe, secure, comfortable or mobile.

If you haven't then you'll need to stock up now, but don't panic. Newspapers like nothing more than publishing scare stories about the costs of modern parenthood and for already-anxious new dads these reports can leave you with visions of a future on the breadline.

In reality babies continue to be born and even baby booms continue to happen regardless of the economic climate.

People keep on having kids and, while many of us do feel the strain financially at times, the benefits of having children and the joy they bring us (most of the time at least) usually makes the sacrifice seem worthwhile.

Here's the kind of thing I mean: a survey in April 2013 by the Centre for Economics and Business Research claimed that it'll cost £220,000 to raise just the one child from birth until they're 21.

If you're buying them a new iPad at every birthday, leaving them with a full-time nanny for half the year and holidaying in Monte Carlo the rest of the time then maybe that figure is bang on the money.

But these surveys are designed to get publicity and create headlines like 'The Soaring Cost of Raising Kids', etc. In reality, while you may well feel a squeeze on your finances with an additional mouth (or two) to feed – you will find a way through it. And it won't demand that you conjure up an additional £10k a year for the next 21 years to do so (though things may get a bit pricey come university time).

So, before you start looking to see if your baby came with a refundable receipt or you contemplate selling your vital organs to pay for the latest fashionable collapsible buggy, take note of how you can best find ways to afford your baby.

BUYING BABY GEAR

WHERE CAN I GET GOOD BABY GEAR TO FIT MY BUDGET?

Unlike adult clothes, accessories and toys, many items of baby stuff don't really suffer much in the way of wear and tear. This is usually because a kid will seemingly grow out of things before the credit card bill for them has even arrived.

As a result you get a shed-load of second-hand gear that's in very good condition and that will one day fill your own shed. For now, however, it will fill a practical function – saving you time and, more crucially, money. Of course you or your partner (much more likely your partner) may insist that your little prince or princess only has the very best of new baby gear – in which case you may well need the wallet of an oligarch. But otherwise check out these places for the tools of the parenting trade.

'Nearly new' baby sales

Does what it says on the label. There's no shame in picking up almost pristine baby grows, booties or even a buggy for up to a tenth of the original cost. Your baby won't care, that's for sure.

The NCT (National Childbirth Trust), a parent-support charity, knock out everything from prams and toys to changing mats and clothes at their massively popular sales. Once you've drawn up your list of essentials and made a rough estimate of the prices you'll pay for new stuff, then seek out the next nearly new sale in your area because the chances are you'll get it all for a third of the original price. (Visit the NCT website, and tap in your postcode to find out when and where the next jumble-sale-style new parents gathering will be: www.nct.org.uk/in-your-area/event-finder)

eBAY/Gumtree/Preloved

Okay, you're having to go by the thumbnail picture on the website, which often reveals more about the seller's hideous home décor than the actual product – but the online auction site is still a useful place to save some cash when 'nesting'. (That's what new mums call buying a houseful of junk for a baby.) For example, in researching the cost of becoming a father I found a double-seated pushchair (for twins) that would have been £220 on offer for just £50 and a BabyDan changing unit which sold for new at £220 – up for grabs at bids starting from £4.99!

The downside of online buying of stuff like cots and buggies is that it won't fit in a post box. Weigh up the pros and cons of driving to collect stuff. If you're still getting a bargain then get bidding. Also take a look at Freecycle.org – an online gathering where people offer unwanted stuff for free in a bid to recycle toys, baby clothes, etc.

Comparison and mother-and-baby websites

Another bonus side to the Internet for expectant fathers (there are many but we won't go into some of the more lurid ones right now) are the message boards. Websites as varied as Mumsnet.com and www.comparestoreprices.co.uk will carry product reviews of items you're looking to buy – featuring comments and useful, honest, bullshit-free reviews.

Wisdom of Fathers

Best Baby Buys ...

'The best product we've bought is the BabaBing FlipOut changing mat – it's brilliant.' Sunil, father of Rita

'Beco Gemini baby carrier. Definitely. It's a soft carrier that can go on your front or back. It folds up very small and we take it everywhere. Elias has been to the shops, the park and Alpine peaks in it.' Mike, father of Elias

'We bought our baby a Bright Starts activity and play mat-cum-gym when she was about six weeks old. This has definitely been the best purchase we made for Niamh so far. It has encouraged independent play and helped her develop her hand–eye co-ordination. The placement of the toys hanging over the mat has encouraged her to roll both ways and when she wasn't particularly mobile we could leave her on it and know she was safe while we got on with other stuff. The toys are interchangeable and you can replace them, which keeps her interested in it – so much so that she still plays with it now at six months old.' Conan, father of Niamh at six months

WHAT DO I REALLY HAVE TO BUY FOR A BABY?

The baby product industry is a thriving one. Much of what it offers is practical, helpful, even essential for you to raise your baby. Much more is a load of trendy gimmicks and fashion accessories that play upon the desire to outdo these Joneses or prey upon our fears and ignorance as newbie mommas and papas.

With a bit of luck you'll find that your budget is boosted in a roundabout way by the generosity of friends and relatives. Pretty much every pair of new parents will have something old, something new, something borrowed and something in either blue or pink that's come to their baby via their own mums and dads or from the baby's new aunts, uncles or godparents, etc.

Don't feel awkward about providing a list of stuff you need for people ask 'what can we get your baby?' in the way of gifts for events like the birth or a christening or just a house visit.

Must have ...

Cot bed

Possibly the best idea of the lot – especially if you're on a budget – these are built to last your child from day one until they're around five years old.

As they get older you simply remove the bars and upgrade any 'extras' from early years 'Beatrix Potter bunny mobiles' to an Angry Birds bedspread and pillowcases. You can get a decent second-hand cot bed – but be sure to use a non-toxic paint if you're changing its colour to suit the nursery décor. (Always replace any missing or broken bars and make sure the sides slide and lock safely.) It's best to pick up a new mattress for your cot or cot bed for safety reasons.

From around: A few pounds on a pre-loved website – if you're willing to go and collect a second-hand cot. You can pay up to £280 or more for the likes of a Hogarth 3-in-1.

Clothes/body suits

'Baby grow' is probably the most appropriate moniker for your kid's first clothes since they seem to outgrow these on an almost daily basis. Get at least a dozen to use and wash in the first week.

Other essential items of clothing include vests, little cardigans and an outfit for outdoors. Your baby's body temperature is a scientific phenomenon on its own. 'Layers' will feature a lot in your vocabulary much more too. Most baby grows are gender specific and often have fun patterns, characters, football team crests on them – and most of all they're cheap. As a result, friends and relatives will buy them for your child by the bulk.

From around: £8 for a pack of five (www.johnlewis.com).

Nappies

A must. Babies are only beaten by politicians in their ability to produce an unfeasible amount of crap. Nappies are the best way to deal with it. The type you use will depend upon whether you and your partner want to use disposable or re-useable (previously called terry or washable) ones.

Both have an effect on the environment – the impact of dumping or washing nappies is a topic of much debate and fills pages on websites likes Mumsnet. Both will hit you in the pocket, although in the case of re-useables only once.

New babies need to be changed, on average, 10 times a day. This gradually reduces as they grow – by around 24 months old the potty training should be all the rage in your home and you'll need them much less. Scented nappy bags are handy for disposing of them and help prevent your home smelling so 'ripe' that even the Jehovah's Witnesses don't call round.

From around: £16 for 100 nappies (Tesco.com).

--- *Dad You Know?* ---

Disposables Income

Several studies suggest that using disposable nappies throughout the entire time until a baby is potty trained can set you back around £2–2,500. Re-useable nappies are reported to reduce that outlay by around two-thirds over the same period. Depending on where you live in the UK you may have access to a nappy laundry service like www.cottontails.co.uk that does the dirty work for you.

Bedding

Baby sleeping bags are a safe way of getting them snug. You place your baby in the sleeping bag with their feet end closest to the end of the cot. Unlike having loose blankets or covers, there's no danger of them pulling anything over their heads in the night. (Remember: duvets and pillows are not recommended for your baby until they are one year old because of the threat of suffocation or simply your baby getting too hot.) For similar safety reasons avoid putting soft toys in the cot too. Make sure that you have plenty of sheets plus a mattress protector for your Moses basket or cot too as you will have plenty of midnight bedding changes to endure.

From around: £15 for a baby sleeping Grobag at www.gro-store.co.uk, or baby sleeping bags are now available from most supermarkets and baby departments.

Bottles and steriliser

Some mums will stick to breastfeeding like it's their sole purpose on Earth. Others will continue to do it for a year or more while also expressing milk into bottles – and attracting both admiration and aghast looks in the process. Most mums will give it a shot for the first few months then switch to the bottles as they collapse in a knackered heap complaining of shredded nipples. Fortunately, formula milk is a safe and nourishing option. With that in mind you'll need bottles and a way of keeping them thoroughly clean. The steriliser helps keep milk sterile by using steam to thoroughly clean the bottles – or else bottles can be sterilised via a hot spin in the microwave.

From around: £25 for Dr Brown's Natural Flow Deluxe Microwave Steam Steriliser (www.Boots.com).

Baby monitor

You can get versions that double as temperature gauges, ones with built-in video cameras and many are walkie-talkie types that even clip on to your belt in case you spend most nights aimlessly wandering around the rooms of your own home wondering how you got into this mess.

There's a lively second-hand baby monitor market on eBay since they're virtually redundant within a few months of your baby being born. Many parents just find the constant vigil of watching the bleeping lights of the monitor – and the resultant paranoia caused by your baby deviously holding its breath – too much to handle.

Others realise that they're only ideal for listening to their partner talking to themselves or breaking wind while they're in the baby's room. Some have discovered that these monitors come into their own when you take your baby away to a hotel with you – ideally a hotel with thin walls and a decent bar.

From around: £35 for a Motorola Digital Baby Monitor (www.mamasandpapas.com).

Pushchair or buggy

This mammoth piece of kit is something you've probably already agonised over, researched, and stopped strangers in the street to try to track down the perfect wheels for your new arrival. From complex travel systems to fold-away pushchairs, it's a whole new world out there. A mad, mad world. See Chapter 5 for more information about the options, but for now be sure that you have something to convey your baby from A to B. Right from the start, it will be crucial that you and your partner can get safely out and about with Baby blissfully unaware of the effort involved.

First-aid kit

Plan ahead. It's unlikely that you will need much in the way of plasters and tinctures for a while, but if you don't get a few basics in then it's guaranteed that you will be sent out at some point in the dead of the night to look for a 24-hour supermarket or petrol station that might just stock baby paracetamol, teething powders or nappy rash cream. Save yourself the hassle – see Chapter 7 for what you may need.

Should have ...

Moses basket

It doesn't float, nor is it especially camouflaged against bulrushes, but this little basket may well be your baby's main form of sleeping arrangement for the first couple of months. (Although your partner's breast may prove to be equally as comfortable for them.)

As it's recommended that your baby sleeps in the same room as you for the first six months, a Moses basket can be an ideal bed if space is tight. The baskets are carried around and then placed on their own 'collapsible' stand. (The word collapsible doesn't feel right when talking about a baby's sleeping arrangements, does it?)

From around: £34.99 at www.mothercare.com or as little as £2 (starting bid) for a used one on eBay.

Baby bath

Babies love a skinny dip in the tub almost as much as a pair of consenting adults, and you can go from using a bowl at first to a simple plastic tub or moulded bath support – right through to a specially designed non-slip mat – called an Aqua pod – which supports your baby once they can sit up in the bath (from about six months). Alternatively you could just wash them in the shower with you or in the sink until they're old enough to be embarrassed by it. (See 'What's the Best Way to Bath Your Baby' in Chapter 1.)

From around: £14.99 for a Winnie the Pooh baby bath (www.mothercare.com).

Room thermometer

Being too hot or too cold in bed is no fun for us adults. For babies it can be equally as bad – only they're not in a position to drag a fan into their bedroom or cuddle up to the cat for warmth. You can get a Philips AVENT Baby digital baby bath and bedroom thermometer for £12.50 that will also gauge the water temperature for your kid's bath water too. According to the Lullaby Trust the bedroom should be kept between 16–20 °C (61–68 °F)so 18 °C (65 °F) is ideal. Alternatively the Grobag Egg Room Thermometer acts as a night light and emits warning colours if the temperature gets too hot or cold (£15.49 at www.mothercare.com).

Car seat

You can get your baby's car seat from high street outlets such as Halfords, Mothercare and the John Lewis Partnership – or online though websites belonging to the major brands such as Britax, Graco and Maxi Cosi. As with all the 'larger' child accessories – buggies, cots, babysitters – it's a good idea to compare prices.

Buying it from the high street store allows you to manhandle the goods and there should be a specialist expert on hand to show you how to fit it and point out the various extras or differences between the styles. If there isn't then ask to see one – fitting these can be fiddly. See Chapter 5 for precise details as to what is required at each stage/age and the options available.

Well, you could have ...

Changing bag and changing mat

You and your partner may already have a baggage collection that's on a par with Heathrow but these purpose-built, multi-pocketed carryalls are *a la mode* these days – and just really useful for hauling around all the stuff you need.

Leaving the house will take on the logistics of a military invasion when you become a dad, so a bag that you can pack for outside is a real plus. There's also a range of fashion, record carrier-style versions for chaps too. These are now up there with the baby carrier as a modern dad's essential and are a much more stylish option than ramming everything in a carrier bag.

From around: £40 for a Silver Cross changing bag in blazer blue (with changing mat); £14 for a travel changing mat at www.johnlewis.com

Cot

Also called a bassinet bed (by Americans mainly but it's becoming more common over here now), a cot is an alternative option to the Moses basket – a more rigid set-up that you don't use to carry the baby around the house in the same way as the basket. Rocking cots can be especially good for getting your baby off to 'bub-byes'. The rocking and the motion have a calming effect.

From around: £39 at www.mothercare.com or £10 second hand on www.preloved.co.uk

Changing table

There's a bit more to these than it initially sounds. Okay, admittedly it's a table that you plonk your baby on to change their nappy or dress them. Some of them are simply flat boards that can attach to the top of a cot.

Others come in the shape of a full set of hand drawers with an oversized top surface area. A changing table will save you a lot of backache as you're able to change your baby at waist level – plus it doubles as decent storage space for their room for a good few years. A personal tip is to avoid putting any shelves directly above the changing table – if you want to avoid spilling anything on to your baby – or if you just value your own skull.

You can of course use the floor to do all this. (It's a much safer move too – since holding your baby in place with one hand while rifling through drawers for baby wipes certainly is far from 'best practice' in the eyes of most midwives.)

From around: £29 for an IKEA Sniglar table; up to £265 for Foppapedretti Rollino Changing Table from wayfair.com, which comes with its own chest of drawers and wheels to move it more easily.

Mobiles

Not an early introduction into the world of text messaging, but a moving, soothing decorative arrangement that dangles over the cot and hypnotises your newborn. Colourful, musical ones keep your kid surprisingly entertained in the early days when they have the recall of a goldfish.

From around: £27.95 for a Thing.a.Majig Safari Musical Mobile at www.amazon.co.uk – though many similar ones can be found on eBay and the like with starting prices of around £2.

Baby carrier

Although not an essential by any means, a baby carrier or sling is a great buy – not just for out and about, though for that reason alone they are worth the money. But whether it's for dad and junior outings and walks or to comfort a colicky baby around the house, 'wearing' your little one is a great way to bond and enjoy time together.

Dad You Know?

Whatever ...

It's not all rosy – 40 per cent of new parents experience feelings of indifference towards their new baby. While paternal detachment is a lot more common than many may think, it's not destined to stay that way. US researchers found that many dads especially experience a delay in bonding with their children shortly after they are born.

But fathers do respond to the interactive qualities of kids and the experts found that when new dads start to sense something coming back from the child, that connection builds and the indifference fades. The best way to kick off this bond the researchers found is through the day-to-day routine of sitting with your child, holding the baby, feeding them – even when you're scared to death of him or her at first.

WHAT USEFUL 'APPS' ARE OUT THERE FOR NEW DADS?

While we're writing the shopping list ... are you looking to load up your mobile phone with some useful, family-focused applications? Here are a few you may want to look into:

NCT babychange

Available for both Android and iPhone. Helps dads find the nearest baby-changing facility, whether you search by town, city or postcode. (Mothercare, Costa and even McDonald's are often sure-fire bets for any off-street nappy changing you need to do.)

British Red Cross Baby and Child First Aid app

This features advice and skills that only take a few minutes to learn but could save a life – www.redcross.org.uk/babyandchildapp

Baby monitor and alarm

This way you can use your smartphone as a baby monitor when you are in another room. This app sends alerts to another phone when the baby wakes.

iBaby Activity Tracker

Useful for the control-freak father (or the forgetful one more likely), you can log when your baby eats, sleeps, uses their nappy and takes medicine, as well as recording their growth. Download from the app store at https://play.google.com

Childcare UK

Application linked to the website www.childcare.co.uk, which is a source of information about local childcare, nurseries and babysitters.

WOWDAD maps

Designed to help dads find child-friendly places around the UK with info on more than 13,000 places from baby-changing facilities, children's clothing shops, eateries that are buggy-friendly or play areas that are soft-padded for toddlers. It is available as a free download from the App Store, for iPhone and iPod Touch.

MadeForMums

This parenting website has launched a free baby weaning app in association with Heinz Baby. It offers a daily meal planner for every meal for the first six months of your baby's introduction to the world of food and is now available on iOS for iPhone and iPad devices.

HEALTH

WHAT CAN WE DO TO GUARD AGAINST COT DEATH?

Sudden infant death syndrome (SIDS) or cot death is a rare occurrence. According to The Lullaby Trust (www.lullabytrust.org.uk) around 290 babies die suddenly and unexpectedly every year in the UK.

It's estimated that 72 per cent of all unexplained deaths occur in babies aged less than four months and since parents have been following the expert advice on ways to reduce the risk of cot death the number of babies dying has fallen by over 70 per cent. To provide your baby with a safe sleeping environment and give you and your partner some peace of mind too, take the following steps:

- Put your baby on their back to sleep – not on their front or side.
- Place them as far down the cot as you can to cut the risk of them wriggling beneath their covers.
- Don't smoke. (Ideally you avoided smoking around your partner when she was pregnant – certainly don't smoke in the same room as your baby now.)
- Lullaby Trust advice says that the safest place for your baby to sleep is in a cot in a room with you for the first six months.
- Don't put your baby's cot next to a radiator. Don't let them get too hot, and keep your baby's head uncovered

when sleeping. The temperature of a baby's sleeping area should be 16–20 °C (61–68 °F), so 18 °C (65 °F) is ideal.

- Avoid falling asleep on the sofa or in an armchair with your baby and resist the urge to put your baby in bed with you.
- Remove all soft objects from your baby's cot – that includes pillows, blankets, animals (stuffed toy ones and real, furry meowing ones).

Dad You Know?

Chemistry Sex

Are you finding it soothing having your baby sleeping in the same room as you? Do you find yourself experiencing a warm, empathetic glow when holding your snoozing nipper? That's because babies and dads experience a biological change when in each other's dozing company.

A study of 362 new dads from the University of Notre Dame shows that dads who sleep near their children experience a drop in testosterone – suggesting this is nature's way of making men more responsive to their children's needs and helping them focus on the demands of parenthood.

'Research has shown that when men become fathers, their testosterone decreases, sometimes dramatically, and that those who spend the most time in hands-on care had lower testosterone,' explained anthropologist Lee Gettler. The new research shows that night-time closeness or proximity between fathers and their kids has effects on men's biology – softening the dad up for his new role.

WHAT IS COLIC ALL ABOUT?

Communication from your baby to you will continue to follow a familiar theme:

Baby wants you to know	How it tells you
They're hungry	Cries
They're tired	Cries
Their nappy needs changing	Cries
They're too hot/cold	Cries
They've got colic	Cries a lot

Colic is the medical professional's way of saying 'that baby won't stop crying'. Even though your little boy or girl will be otherwise in perfect health, they appear to be seriously dischuffed about something. It's no consolation for you or your partner as your newborn bawls the walls down but, if you can, take some comfort in the knowledge that it's a very common condition that affects one in five babies, according to NHS data.

With colic, despite the crying, your baby should carry on feeding and gaining weight healthily. It's just that they tend to spend much of the time when they're not eating or sleeping lying with their legs in the air, screaming – no matter what their frantic parents try to do to comfort them.

New mums are often advised to try a few different ploys to combat colic including simply burping their baby through to changing their diet – if they're breastfeeding – to eliminate possible colic-causing foods such as caffeine or dairy.

New dads can help with a few tried-and-tested methods including:

- **Keeping the noise down:** More specifically helping to make a calm, 'womb-like' feel to their environment. Maybe subdue the lighting and put some calming sounds on an MP3 player or iPod ... like you and your partner used to before Baby came along.
- **Take them out:** Motion can have an almost hypnotic effect on some crying babies so taking them out for a stroll in

the buggy or just walking them around the house in your arms may have the desired 'chillaxing' effect.

- **Do the bath thing:** You may be getting to be a dab hand at bathing your baby by now – whether you are or not, try giving your baby a warm bath to ease their colicky cries.
- **Get to burp:** Dads make good burpers – in more ways than one. Burping your baby is one way of easing your baby's gripes and so cutting down on the all-round distress of colic.

Wisdom of Fathers

Sleep Pattern

'I don't feel anything has hit me too hard really. The sleep deprivation was initially the toughest part, as I'm someone who needs a solid eight hours to be able to function properly. I sleep in the spare room during the week now so I can be effective at work, so that's not too bad. I read a couple of books about what to expect, and that really opened my eyes to what was coming.' Michael, father of Jemima at four weeks

---

WHAT'S THE BIG DEAL ABOUT SETTING A 'ROUTINE'?

'The Routine!' In your pre-parenting days this probably meant nothing at all. Those new parents neurotically babbling on about not upsetting their baby's feed-sleep-poo-feed body clock probably seemed a bit too strung out in your naïve opinion. But now you've joined the secret society you will be enlightened by this crucial and highly effective piece of baby psychology.

A typical baby routine can be steadfastly stuck to by parents who realise that the repetition and simple sequences of events provides security and stability, for all parties. It's a case of trial and error for most parents but once you've got a running order of what works best for the day then you, as dad, can help take over with tasks and more crucially enable yourself and your partner to manage your time more effectively.

It's probably worth jotting down your baby's routine at first to help stick to it – at around eight weeks that routine will probably look something along the lines of this:

Example of a Typical Rug-Rat's Routine*

05:30 – Baby wakes and wants a feed – then nods off again.

08:30ish – Baby's up again for more of the same – possibly the second nappy change of the day too.

9:00 – Baby crashes out once more.

10:30 – Guess what? Baby's up for a feed and change and now some play time, possibly a walk outside to provide much-needed stimulation for mum.

12:30 – Nap time for baby.

14:30 – Wake time for baby. Accompanied by feed and play and possibly another walk for sanity's sake.

16:00 – Nap time.

18:30 – Feed, change, burp, bath – a sequence most men can recognise, this one's for baby though. Followed by getting baby changed and in bed.

21:00 – Wake up baby for first night feed.

Of course this is a basic example and far too precise and clear-cut to bear much resemblance to reality, but you get the idea. Waking, feeding, changing, putting back to sleep again is pretty much the drill at this time of their lives. As a dad you'll soon be made aware of the importance of the routine and how it will end up structuring your lives for the next few months.

The great thing about working to the routine is that, if it's a schedule you know you can stick to, the baby generally adapts to it quickly and you can include more of the everyday things you need or want to do in your lives around it. Knowing your baby will most likely nap for 90 minutes at a set time each day can make it easy to catch up on whatever stuff you've been missing out on as a couple since the baby came along – catching up with people, doing work or whiling away time on Facebook, watching a film you recorded ... I'll let you fill in the blanks.

* Times will vary according to make, model and method of fuelling for baby.

Why do babies need to be fed at night?

Part of the routine for your baby will also feature night-time feeds. From birth until they're at least a couple of months old most babies will wake up a couple of times in the night for a feed.

As they get a bit older – say around three months onwards – this should reduce down to just the one night feed. More often than not babies at six months will start to settle into a sleep pattern that means they don't wake for a feed in the middle of the night.

Sometimes they may just get thirsty or wake because they're teething, cold or unwell.

What are baby- or parent-led routines?

The routine or schedule is such a crucial part of the early days of parenthood that it divides opinion and has led to the establishment of several schools (or possibly academies these days) of thought about what's best for Baby. There are those who advocate, pontificate and generally bang on about baby-led routines and on the other side those who insist the only way to go is with parent-led routines.

The first one – surprise, surprise – is dictated by what your baby wants. It's a routine that was espoused by a Dr Spock (honest) in a book called *The Common Sense Book of Baby and Child Care.*

Spock's logic says that parents can learn to recognise signs of what is needed in the way of feeds, naps, play, etc. Proponents of this method say parents can steer their babies a little – e.g. encourage them to take a morning and an afternoon nap, but not set a strict daily agenda.

Parent-led routines on the other hand are the type that have made maternity-nurse-cum-baby-guru Gina Ford a household name. This approach says that parents shouldn't rely solely on their baby's demands for feeds – because they may mis-read the signs and be almost constantly feeding their baby, leading to exhausted parents, or else newborn babies may go underfed because they don't wake to signal feeds. These routines build in regular feeds and naps to allow for a more regulated day and night.

HOW DOES ONE WET ONE'S BABY'S HEAD?

Once the seemingly sole reserve of the un-reconstructed alpha male, the celebration that is 'wetting the baby's head' is now an egalitarian, fun-for-all-the-family event. When the time is right new mums get just as pissed as new dads to honour the arrival of their offspring – barbecues or christenings often form a backdrop to this.

You may even decide to make it a shared event or even throw the house open to all friends and family, prospective godparents and your soon-to-be-ex next door neighbours. If nothing else, the head-wetting serves the purpose of letting every new dad know that babies and hangovers really don't mix.

In the main and just like weddings, funerals and major football successes, the birth of a child remains established as a reason for many a British male at least to 'get on it'. If you're really into breaking new ground as a 21st-century father then a drink with some of the other fathers on the antenatal course you attended could be a good chance to share experiences or swap 'girl' stuff or 'boy' stuff if you made the wrong prediction.

HOW DO WE REGISTER THE BIRTH?

Congratulations! Amidst all this hullabaloo you may have missed the chance to congratulate yourself for becoming a new father. Now, just to make things all nice and official you need to register your baby as, well, your baby.

As new parents you need to do this within six weeks – or 42 days to be precise – of the birth at your nearest Registry Office. You'll find this listed in the phonebook, on your local authority website or at www.ukbmd.org.uk

If you're not married, the mother must register the birth – if she wants the father's name to appear on the birth certificate then the father must go along too.

If you're married then you can register the birth yourself.

You need to tell them:

- The date and place of your child's birth.
- The forename, middle name/s and surname that you've chosen for them.
- The name, birth date, place of birth and occupation of the father.
- The name, birth date, place of birth and occupation of the mother.

In return for exposing your little one to their first dealings with state bureaucracy you'll get: a birth certificate for your child, which in turn will open up a whole new world of red tape and bureaucracy to them.

It'll also mean they can be registered with a GP and ensure they're able to access any benefits or state support they're entitled to. And it means you have written proof that 'You are the Daddy'.

WHAT IS CHILD BENEFIT?

Child Benefit is a state allowance paid towards child provision for new parents. It's paid weekly – the rate for the eldest or only child is £20.30 per week as at August 2013. Benefit for additional children is £13.40 per child. It's paid into your bank account every four weeks – though you can get it paid weekly if you're a single parent or have certain other benefits. To get more information contact your local government benefits department or go online to www.hmrc.gov.uk/childbenefit

Wisdom of Fathers

First Few Months

'It's a great time. The best things at this moment are Logan's smiles – especially first thing in the morning. They break my heart every time he does them. Also seeing him grow and develop on a day-by-day basis. He is making more and more noises and trying to grab things and supporting himself on his legs. I really enjoy bathtime with him too, probably as that is really our time together and it feels really special.' Steve, father of Logan at four months

3 JUGGLING ACTS

Child's Life: Weeks 9–12

WHAT'S GOING ON WITH OUR BABY AT THIS STAGE?

From around three months, your bundle of delight may be dabbling in a few of the following traits:

- They may be awake for about 8 to 10 hours a day on average.
- They could be making those gurgling, baby sounds – cooing back at you when you talk to them.
- Smiling. There should be some smiling back at you in recognition and giggling around now.
- Watching and following objects with their eyes – money works well. Also turning toward loud sounds should come naturally now.
- They may be holding their head steady for short times – and could be bringing their hands together.

Wisdom of Fathers

Feed Times

'For the first three months we followed Elias and did what-ever he seemed to want in terms of sleeping and eating. At three months we decided enough was enough and intro-duced feed times and bedtimes. We plan to do some elements of that earlier with our next baby – particularly the idea of a bedtime – and that sleeping is something you do in a dark, quiet place.' Mike, father of Elias

HOW DID THEY SUDDENLY BECOME SO ALERT?

While neither yourself nor your partner will claim to have 'mastered' anything as yet, the chances are that by now the pair of you are jacks of various trades including changing, helping with feeds, soothing, picking up, putting down and changing again. Both of you will have changed in the past couple of months – but we'll come to that later.

Right now your baby's ticking a few milestone boxes. Their motor skills are developing all the time as they grow. Muscles are gaining strength, co-ordination skills are kicking in and your little boy or girl will be making moves all of their own now.

Some of those primitive, instinctive reflexes will still be in place. Your baby will suck on your finger with quite some purchase and force if you let them – they'll find this quite comforting too – though that natural trigger to do this by touch-ing their cheek will begin to fade as they discern the difference between your working man's musty mitts and mum's milk-bearing boob.

By this stage your baby will be much more self-determined when it comes to body movements. They'll hold their head up more steadily and keep it straight too.

WHAT'S A GOOD TOY FOR A BABY AT THIS TIME?

Although they're still too young to play with toys as such at two months, those fun soft play mats you can buy for babies (Blossom Farm Baby Gym, £20 at www.mothercare.com) can be a good starter at this age. Play gyms are soft and brightly coloured with head rests and sometimes feature lullaby music devices. The key thing at this point though is their hanging toys that dangle above them from a Wembley arch-like arrangement. These are great for engaging and helping them activate their focus and grip – they're also easy to transport (the mat, not the baby) and thankfully they're washable too. During the early rounds of visits to friends and family they'll make for a handy base camp for your baby.

WHEN WILL WE GET A DECENT NIGHT'S SLEEP?

Your baby's sleep patterns are evolving – even though yours may be going into meltdown. Usually they'll still be kipping on and off, sporadically, for up to 16 hours a day – and by sporadic it means they're not guaranteed to be sleeping all through the night yet. Breastfed babies have a habit of waking every three hours or so for some tucker too – but they're getting into feeding routines so their sleep will become less disruptive ... for everyone!

- Agree a rota that works best for you both – and if that means Dad doing two nights of bottle feeds so that mum gets a refreshing sleep through then give it a try.
- Or else maybe try an 'evening shift' that one of you does and an 'early morning' shift that the other partner takes on with a view to sharing the night shift. Be prepared for patterns to break – usually just when you think your baby is set in its sleeping ways.
- Learn to cat-nap. Don't be afraid to try a little meditation even and say 'sod the housework'. Sleep deprivation can

put serious strain on an already challenging situation so be prepared to put your and your partner's rest high on the list of priorities for a while.

Wisdom of Fathers

Habit Forming

'The biggest mistake we made was not getting Baby into a routine early – not anything particularly complex, but a basic routine. Also, we didn't really research what the better feeding bottles were, so when Baby didn't latch on to the breast we had to go and buy some quickly, and have recently (after doing some research) bought a different brand.' Sunil, father of Riya

---

WHY DOES OUR BABY NEED MORE VACCINATIONS?

At this stage your baby will have the last batch of the early vaccinations – don't worry, unlike haircuts you won't be doing these yourself. This is the last round they will have until they reach one year old when they'll have to go through a few more.

At this point they'll be having a second and third dose of the 5-in-1 vaccine, also a meningitis jab (split into two doses), a second dose of rotavirus vaccination and pneumococcal. It's a tough time for your little one and many parents find it equally distressing seeing their baby in pain.

If you're able to go along and support both your baby and your partner – or if needs be take your baby into the clinic yourself to save your partner some of the emotional pain – try to do so.

YOUR RELATIONSHIP

WHAT'S HAPPENING WITH OUR RELATIONSHIP?

Be prepared for the stress of new parenthood to put a big strain on your relationship with your partner. For new mums the first child can have a dramatic effect on their self-esteem as well as everything else. If your wife or partner is working it can be especially tough trying to deal with the dramatic change to their circumstances. From being in control in their job and having a routine and agenda that they set, they suddenly find themselves at the beck and call of their newborn baby.

It's a confusing time for new parents – especially with so many varied opinions on how best to raise a baby coming from friends, family and the media. Many new mums, unsurprisingly, will question their own methods and feelings – no matter how realistic she is, she may wonder why some days she just can't face being a new mum. Don't be surprised if at the end of an exhausting emotional day spent worrying about the baby, its feeding, if it's warm enough and comparing herself with other mums, that the strain spills over into rows and bad moods.

Dad You Know?

Domestic Blitz

Parents who suffer from marital instability may set their infants up for sleep troubles in toddlerhood, according to research published in May 2011 in the journal *Child Development*. The study found that a troubled marriage when a baby is 9 months old contributes to trouble sleeping when the child is 18 months of age. It may be that troubled houses are stressful houses, and that stress is the cause of the sleep problems.

New dads will struggle at times trying to get to grips with the change in the dynamics of their relationship. There's a whole new focus now and priorities of time, attention and money will shift. New dads need to know that their partners may be going through the following too:

- **Self-questioning:** Wondering if they're failing as a mother because their baby isn't following the textbook development stages or doesn't do what her friend's baby does or isn't looking or acting like the baby in the adverts.
- **Baby bombshells:** Babies have a fantastic ability to completely embarrass parents in public. Your partner may have had a day where your little 'un has thrown up, screamed to get away from its grandma, pooed before it had a nappy on or thrown food all over its mum ... or all of these together.
- **Wondering about work No.1:** For all those pre-birth intentions she may have had about going back to the office and resuming her career at the end of her maternity leave – she may now be thinking 'I can't leave my baby!!!!' And she may be wondering how to break this to you.
- **Wondering about work No.2:** She can't wait to get back there and wants you to take over the childcare so she can ... and may be wondering how to break *this* to you.

In most cases new dads can play a supportive role by stepping into her shoes as often as possible and spending time with the baby. You'll build up plenty of empathy at least. Don't try to come up with answers or quick-fix solutions when she's bawling her eyes out – as tempting as it may be to go down this tried-and-tested male route. Comfort her as best you can and then, when you feel the time is right (i.e. Baby's asleep and you're both fed and relaxed), try talking through her concerns and discussing what her plans are at this stage. And, just like your little baby, be prepared for any plans you have to need changing regularly.

--- *Wisdom of Fathers* ---

Family Strain

'I felt like a robot for six to seven weeks of just continuous washing, dishes, cooking, cleaning – trying to support my wife as best as possible while she struggled with the feeding and emotional issues.' Tom, father of Lewis.

'There were times when both of us would have gladly taken our son and put him on the neighbour's doorstep – at the time you think that they're never going to sleep through and the strain is tough. But after around seven weeks he was going down for five to six hours solid – that was bliss.' Keiran, father of Jake and Reuben

CAN WE HAVE SEX AGAIN NOW?

A 2013 study published in *BJOG: An International Journal of Obstetrics and Gynaecology* found that by around six weeks after the birth just over 40 per cent of first-time mothers (who'd had a vaginal birth) had had sex again. This figure was a lot less for women who'd had an episiotomy (cut and repair of the tissue between the vagina and anus ... if you were wondering). By 12 weeks after the birth that had risen to 78 per cent.

Your partner will need to physically and emotionally heal before she can enjoy sex again. The pair of you may need to psychologically mend a little too – witnessing a birth can scar a man (temporarily) and put him off the idea of sex for a while.

In fact a study carried out by University of Michigan researchers and also published in 2013 says that dads may be just as worried about renewing sexual activity because they are often tired and feel sidelined by the new addition to the family. The survey found that around one in five new fathers did not resume lovemaking for more than three months. One in three reported making love to their wives in the first six weeks, with a similar proportion having sex between seven and 12 weeks. Among the reasons cited for delay was concern about the woman's physical condition following childbirth – and a lack of time. Of all 114 new dads who responded to this particularly nosey investigation, 82 per cent of them said they'd had sex with their partner again 12 weeks after the baby was born.

When you do resume 'normal service' you'll need to handle her with care in the bedroom, on the sofa or over the dining table at first – especially if she's breastfeeding. Take precautions too – if you're not planning on having another child before your first one's even started walking then you should use whatever birth control methods tick your box. It's not impossible for a woman to conceive again shortly after having a child – in fact she can get pregnant even if she hasn't started her periods again yet. She may have problems using birth control devices and may not be able to use the pill either when she's breastfeeding – so perhaps use a condom for now.

Why doesn't she feel like having sex again just yet?

If you want to understand how a woman might feel about sex after she's given birth, think about why people have sex. 'Physical pleasure, intimate connection, the desire to give, because they feel horny,' suggests Siski Green – mother, sex writer and author of How to blow her mind in Bed. 'Almost all of these reasons are null and void for her right now. For physical pleasure she has your baby. Every time she cuddles your baby her body releases similar chemicals to when she orgasms.'

Some women have enough love and generosity left over after they've changed nappies, fed and burped their baby, sneaked a power nap and had a cup of tea, to want to make you feel good too.

'Most women don't have enough energy left to have sex just for your satisfaction. So you're left with feeling horny.

Chances are, what with being absolutely exhausted, having a still-bloated post-pregnancy body, potentially sore or injured genitals, being horny is about as far from her reality as the idea of taking her newborn baby skydiving. It's not even on her radar right now.'

Why she doesn't feel sexy then?

Her day-to-day activities are hardly stimulating. 'Poo. Wee. Puke. Reading about fluffy rabbits and bears. Singing lullabies. None of it is arousal-inducing,' says Green. 'Plus she's just plain exhausted. It's not sexy to feel so tired you can barely make it to the bed to sleep.'

There are also plenty of physical changes that, however common and expected they were, are still pretty depressing:

- During pregnancy her hair got thicker – fewer hairs fell out. After pregnancy the opposite occurs. 'Although her hair will most likely get back to its pre-pregnancy state at some point, grabbing clumps of hair every time you wash or brush it and feeling how much thinner your hair is, is terrifying,' says Green.
- Even if she's not breastfeeding, her breasts will change shape and size as a result of pregnancy – as will her stomach. 'It's been stretched like a balloon and needs time to get back to normal. It may never do that. And that funny dark line that she got during pregnancy? It's still there! It takes months to disappear for some women,' explains Green.
- Stretchmarks. 'They're everywhere,' says Green. Also her clothes could be an issue. 'Nothing fits, not even her maternity clothes – they're now shapeless and baggy, and she can't get her pre-pregnancy clothes over the top of her huge breasts or hips.'
- There's probably one outfit that she fits into and she's wearing it every day. 'The sexy little bras and knickers she loved so much feel uncomfortable on her new post-pregnancy

body, so she's sticking to comfortable M&S cotton stuff –
comfy not sexy,' adds Green.

WHAT CAN I DO TO RESTORE OUR SEX LIFE AFTER BABY?

Tips for getting back on the horse, so to speak, usually revolve
around being patient and letting your partner heal – emotionally and physically. Pushing sex back on to the agenda when she
doesn't feel like it will just create tension at a time when things
are already tough. Instead try to:

Do mummy massage to make sure you stay physically connected

'It's really important if you're going to get back to something
like a normal sex life,' says Green. So while she's not feeling up
for sex, give plenty of cuddles and massages. It'll relax her,
she'll feel loved and the massage will help you feel emotionally
connected.

Bring back memories

Somehow you have to remind her of how you felt about her
pre-pregnancy and how she felt about you. 'Think about how
you used to treat her body or how you used to look at her – did
you sometimes squeeze her behind when she was in the kitchen,
admire her slim waist or pert nipples, or grab a handful of
breast when no one was looking? That's the kind of mindset
you need to get back into,' suggests Green. Of course, grabbing
body parts might not go down so well, especially if she's in the
middle of some child-related activity – or Tesco – so think of
other ways to show her that you still see her as the sexy attractive woman you knew before pregnancy.

Remind her of sexy times you spent together

'Do this at a time when sex isn't an option so it doesn't seem as though you're only trying to point out that you're not having sex right now,' says Green. 'Remind her of something she used to wear. Tell her about a piece of clothing she wore that you loved and explain why. Buy her new underwear.' If you can't buy it yourself, get her a voucher or enlist the help of a relative/friend (hers, not yours!).

BUT ONCE WE START AGAIN ALL WILL BE FINE, RIGHT?

Even when sex is back on the scene, be aware of a few potential pitfalls you'll want to avoid ...

Smooth things along

Her breasts will feel sore and her vagina may be drier as a side effect of the lactation process – couples are often advised to use a lubricating jelly during sex. For some new mums oestrogen and progesterone production takes a while to get back to normal after birth – they may not experience periods for many months. And, if their oestrogen production isn't back to normal, their bodies won't respond to arousal in the same way – the vagina may not lubricate itself as it usually does. 'Lubrication doesn't need to be in the KY Jelly form – there are some great massage-and-lubrication creams and gels that you can use to rub all over each other, making it feel less clinical and more fun,' suggests Green.

Look out for leaks

Her breasts, when stimulated, may leak some milk too – be prepared for that and the fact that many women report enjoying sex more after having their first child!

Better be safe

Still take precautions – and don't believe that old wives' tale that a breastfeeding woman can't get pregnant.

BABYCARE

HOW CAN I GET OUR BABY LOOKING GOOD?

Now is a good time to add a few more dad skills to your armoury. Along with all that growth that's going on with your baby, and the resultant weighing and measuring and plotting of percentiles, their hair and their fingernails are growing too. This is where the steady hand of the metrosexual stylist that is the modern dad comes to the fore – that's right, what better than the steady hand of the reliable, relaxed father to do the grooming?

How do I cut my baby's fingernails?

- Use special baby scissors (baby nail clippers and scissors set, £3.05 at www.boots.com).
- Have Mum hold and distract Baby while you try not to tickle them (Baby, that is).
- Carefully clip each one (it may help if it's during feeding time as they're doubly distracted).
- Don't force it if they start getting agitated, go back and do the rest later.

How do I cut my baby's hair?

Maybe it's for a photo or a special occasion, or just because they're starting to appear like they're in the Coldstream Guards but at some point your baby will need a bit of home barbering.

Okay you could take them to a salon but think of the rigmarole of packing everything on to the buggy, the struggle to keep them *in situ* while the hairdresser asks them what holidays they have planned ... and most of all think of the cost. To cut your baby's hair you will need:

- **Consent:** Of your wife/partner to cut the baby's hair. Most men will have no prior experience of this (clipping some chewing gum out of the dog's matted fur doesn't count) so be prepared to have to put forward a reasoned argument as to why you should suddenly be let loose on your baby's locks.
- **Clippers:** Don't even think about using actual sharp scissors to cut a baby's hair. You can get specialist baby hair clippers or simply use a pair of your own if you have them with the setting to the length you want to trim to.
- **Distraction:** Mum could be there to distract baby – if she can bear to watch this. Or else if they're old enough (like, say, at least a year) give them a snack to chew on while you trim. Or maybe see if they want to watch one of the many 'baby has first haircut' videos on YouTube while you give them a trim.
- **A son:** You'll need one of these because you sure as hell won't be allowed to do this with your daughter's hair.

Dad You Know?

Oh, You Handsome Devil, Daddy

New dads on the other hand should have no fears about how they look. According to a study in 2013 by the University of California, pregnancy and birth can give the effect of boosting male confidence and making them more attractive (albeit only in the mirror). After investigating 200 couples in a study, scientists concluded that having physical proof of virility – aka, your new nipper – may give the male ego a boost. 'For men, having a child may serve to enhance feelings of masculinity, resulting in men feeling more attractive' said researcher Alicia Cast.

Wisdom of Fathers

The Routine

'Get your baby into a routine as early as possible. We found that the key to getting our little girl to sleep is to make sure she feeds properly when she goes to bed – which meant feeding her from a bottle – making sure she drank the lot, and if she didn't, letting her have the rest when she woke up.' Dominic

4 IN AT THE SHALLOW END

Child's Life: Weeks 13–16

WHAT'S HAPPENING WITH OUR BABY AT THIS STAGE?

There's plenty of activity going on right now with your baby as they grow stronger and more co-ordinated by the day. They're becoming more responsive to you too so keep the chat going whenever you're with them. A few 'skills' of theirs you might be able to tick off right now include:

- Holding their head up steadily – it may not seem like much to us 206-boned adults but to a floppy, bones-still-fusing baby it's a landmark move.
- Bearing weight on their legs. This doesn't mean they're anywhere near walking, but if you hold them in the standing position you'll notice that they instinctively take the kind of unsure, wobbly steps most of us do at closing time.
- Reaching out for objects or even grasping at things – like your nose.
- Possibly rolling over when they're on the floor.
- Dribbling – okay, it's not a skill but it's not uncommon for teething to begin as early as four months.

73

- Babies can be making 'cooing' sounds when you talk to them around now. It's a mimicking move as they mirror what you do. You can't understand what they're saying – but they're pretty clueless as to what you're on about too. Those 'coos' will soon convert to 'muma' and 'dada' sounds.

WHY IS THE ROUTINE CHANGING?

As your baby grows so its needs and feeds and sleeping patterns will change too. So that routine you steadfastly obeyed the first few weeks into their life may need something of a re-think four months down the line.

Right now, at around four months their routine could feasibly look something more like this:

06:00 – Baby wakes up, gurgles and makes those lights on the monitor flash.

06:30 – Parent clutching the shortest straw – or Mum if breast is still the breakfast option – does first feed .

07:00–09:00ish – Baby awake, playing and engaging.

09:30 – Baby goes down for a morning nap after a nappy change.

11:00 – Up for a mid-morning feed.

11:30 – Awake and playing or at baby club or out for walk in the buggy.

13:30 – Nap time again after a change of nappy.

15:00 – Up again for more grub and play, maybe another walk out.

16:00 – Yep, you guessed it – nap time. Not a long one, just enough to stop 'em getting mardy.

17:30 – Wake up and scoff. Play and engage – possibly with daddy if he's home from work? Bathtime too and stories ahead of final feed of the day.

19:00 – Final bottle or breastfeed of the day then Baby put to bed for the night.

19:05 – Shiraz or Chardonnay? *pop*. TV. Bed.

Dad You Know?

Toys in their Reach

From four months onwards the combination of their craving for noise and ability to reach out and grasp will make a rattle a toy that they'll really take to.

WHAT'S MY ROLE IN ALL OF THIS?

Bless their cotton booties, your little fella or princess will be getting more playful now as they grow. They could well be rolling around – and you could well still be wondering what your role in all of this is. Over the next few weeks you may find that your baby is noticeably fixing their gaze on objects, grasping them as best they can and more than likely sucking on it. They will react by smiling when you shake a colourful, noisy rattle at them – or may prefer a few moments of their own, seemingly amusing themselves by studying their own foot.

The key thing for new dads is to be able to seize upon this time to start to engage more and more with their child. It's tough – especially if you're working long hours – for dads who are the sole breadwinner at this time to be there. But it's vital that when they are there they get to have fun with their baby. Timing is crucial – babies can get overstimulated at the wrong time or have a greater need for food or sleep at others, but make sure you spend some time every day having fun time together. Don't fret about having toys or following any rules, just relax and laugh with them, lifting them up and down making them smile, tickling their hands and singing them songs – simple but enjoyable for you both.

Wisdom of Fathers

Bonding

'Both my kids loved to touch my stubble (something their mum didn't have thankfully!) and they knew the distinctive differences in our voices from very early on. I'd play with them a bit rougher than their mum did – but that's just a natural thing, not something I consciously did but it all meant they knew the difference between Mummy and Daddy – different people with different bonding processes.' Matt, father of Ruby and Ella

WHAT CAN I DO TO HELP MY BABY'S DEVELOPMENT?

It's still early days in the life of your young Jedi but there's a whole bunch of stuff you can be doing with them even now that'll bring on their cognitive skills, improve their co-ordination and generally cement your bond while keeping you away from less fruitful habits.

Rattle and mum

Keep helping their hand–eye co-ordination with toys like rattles. They'll start transferring it from one hand to the other, partly for their own amusement and in realisation that they have such symmetry – and probably as an attempt to stop you from waving it in their face.

Keep on talking

By this point your baby will home in on the source of a voice – and will apparently easily distinguish Mum's from Dad's. Try having conversations with your baby – saying something and giving them a chance to come up with an 'answer'.

Belly good

Many babies can lay on their belly and lift their head up – around 90 degrees – or even prop themselves up on their forearms at this age. Try this in front of a mirror since your baby will be able to focus on their own reflection at this time too. Encouraging this 'tummy time' will help them to develop their ability to control their head – but they might not necessarily thank you for it.

Get baby bonding

If you weren't already then this is the time to get playing, massaging, bathing and chatting with your baby – and swimming with them.

Weird Things Babies Do

Wind Times ...

Some babies will suffer with bloating if gas become trapped and they're struggling to release it on their own – but laying them on their back and alternately lifting each leg in the air, bending at the knees slightly and/or massaging their belly will often bring on a fart – much to their relief if not necessarily yours.

WHY IS IT SO GOOD TO TAKE MY BABY SWIMMING?

After spending the best part of nine months spinning around in the water-filled sac, it's little wonder that babies generally have a penchant for a pool. From three months onwards is about the time the experts suggest your baby will have grown enough to get an enjoyable, safe experience in the warm bit of your municipal baths.

No bombing, no running, know vaccinations

Many parents will wait until their baby has had its full set of inoculations before taking them along to splash, kick and gurgle their way around a pool that's home to other people's wee. However, the NHS advice says that you can take your baby swimming prior to them having all their jabs. (We're talking chlorinated, clean pools here – save the paddle in the Ganges till later perhaps.)

Warm water babies

Those younger than six months old ideally need a heated pool to play in – their internal body regulator is still at a formative stage so it's best to go to the designated baby pool that should be heated to around 32°C (90°F).

Pack for two

Whereas you may usually take a towel, trunks and enough change for a bag of vending-machine Monster Munch after your dip, you need to go prepared to the baby pool. This can mean taking a warm bottle for feeding after the swim – or a snack when they're a little older and moving on to solids. A towel for your baby – the ones with the towelling hood – add warmth and look cute. Take some of your baby's bathtime toys too. The toys may help your little one feel more at home – and don't forget the obligatory changing mat and nappy bag. And plan for how to juggle Baby and yourself in the changing room – it's best to take in your buggy or car seat so that you have somewhere safe to put Junior when they are dry and dressed.

Keep sessions short

When they're this young it's best not to spend too long in the pool. It's a new experience for you both, babies can get cold very easily and wrinkly babies just look like Benjamin Button. For those babies up to about a year old you should stick to about 30 minutes max – but get out earlier if your baby is shivering.

Join the club

Look in to joining a parent-and-baby swim club if the pool runs one. They're a good way of meeting other new mums and dads – which can often be a useful experience in sharing local knowledge and general baby banter with someone who'll empathise. They can provide some structure to the day for both you and your baby if you're the one doing the bulk of the childcare.

When shouldn't I take them swimming?

Don't take your baby swimming if:

- They've got a bad cold, are running a temperature or have been unwell.
- They've had a stomach upset in the past 48 hours.
- They're showing signs of a skin problem that could be irritated by the chlorine.
- They've brought a note from Mum excusing them.

How do baby swim classes work?

When you sign up for baby swim classes they usually involve a small group of mums and dads – in your swimwear – getting into the junior section of the pool with the babies. If the water feels warm, like someone's peed in it, that's probably because someone has. But also it's meant to be at a temperature that your baby feels comfortable with.

Baby swim teachers will encourage you both to learn through play a bit – though the crux of it is just getting you both to have fun and enjoy time in the water. Some of the little exercises the teacher gets you to do are based upon developing the intuitive reflexes a baby has when plonked in the water; they're natural swimmers. Babies have an inbuilt 'gag reflex' that's strongest up to six months old and allows them to hold their breath under water instinctively.

Wisdom of Fathers

Taking my Baby to the Pool

'I first took Harrison swimming when he was 12 weeks old – with the Little Dippers swim group (based in London and Sussex). I'm a big water fan and wanted to introduce him to the experience when he was very young. At that age they hold no fear, unlike their parents. It was also a really nice way for me to spend some one-on-one time with him, which isn't easy given work commitments. I didn't have any concerns as such – more general apprehension as to how he would react. I quickly discovered that he was more at ease than I thought he would be. That first class is now a total blur; the time goes so quickly. We both thoroughly enjoyed it though, it was great that it was something that we could experience together. It has probably benefitted me more than it has Harrison at this point. I now feel like I'm in control when we're in the water together. I've also realised that babies are actually more robust than I thought.' Kevin, father of Harrison

SHOULD I PLAY MUSIC TO OUR BABY?

Music most definitely strikes a chord with the wee ones. You may well have been laying down some tracks for your baby's enjoyment when they were still in their mum's tum – many a dad does. Whether you did or not, now is as good a time as any to expose them to the eclectic delights of your playlist because:

- Babies pick up on musical and linguistic rhythms – as with foods, the greater variety of notes you expose them to at an earlier age the more they'll enjoy sampling them.
- Babies have 'favourite' tracks – scientists at Paris Descartes University found that one-month-old babies remember music that was played to them in the third trimester of their mothers' pregnancies.
- Playing live music to premature babies has been shown to help some of them sleep better according to a 2013 review of studies from New York hospitals.
- Babies who share music with their parents smile more, communicate better and show earlier and more sophisticated brain responses according to studies published in two journals, *Developmental Science* and *Annals of the New York Academy of Sciences*.

Hold your baby as you're listening to your music, don't be afraid to turn tracks into lullabies and even let them pick up on your dad-dancing rhythm to help you both relax and release some happy hormones.

POSTNATAL DEPRESSION

HOW DO I SPOT POSTNATAL DEPRESSION (PND) IN MY PARTNER?

'When a wife or partner is suffering from postnatal depression it has a massive knock-on effect for the men and husbands,' explains Mark Williams, a father with first-hand experience of postnatal depression. After his wife suffered with PND Mark established a support network for new dads and the partners of sufferers. 'The severity of the depression varies between individuals,' he explains.

'Men can find themselves in the position of having to carry out all the main duties at home, while also working and caring for their wife and newborn child and sometimes other children.'

The focus of the network Williams has established is to provide men who find themselves in the same position he was in with the help and support they need to be able to manage and cope through this difficult time period.

WHAT ARE THE SIGNS NEW DADS SHOULD LOOK OUT FOR?

Indicators that your partner has PND can include some of the following:

- Guilty and ready to blame herself
- Panic attacks
- Exhausted and lack of motivation
- Suicidal feelings
- Very tearful
- Lost confidence
- Lonely
- Doesn't think she is a good mum or can't look after your newborn baby
- Unable to enjoy the new baby
- Changes in sleep pattern and eating habits
- Body language/eye contact changes rapidly.

If a new father feels that their partner may be suffering with postnatal depression, he should talk to the health visitor and get an appointment with the GP. 'Family support is very important, and the quicker you get help, the quicker the recovery,' says Williams. Don't shy away from the issue and try to keep your partner talking about her feelings.

Remember one in seven new mums will have some form of postnatal depression. For many women an initial combination of fatigue, anxiety and trauma can contribute to a condition called 'baby blues'. However, while this is a genuine condition in itself, it's one that refers to the short-term drop in the new mum's mood and feelings of self-esteem just after the baby is born.

Be on guard for the signs of a further, deeper form of depression. As the new dad you'll be the first to witness symptoms – and knowing how to act when you spot them is crucial. Don't be tempted to go down the line so many blokes do and try to offer instant-fix suggestions. Don't hope she'll just 'snap out of it' either.

Your partner may try to hide it for fear of not being seen as a good, coping mother. 'Remember you know if she is acting out of sorts,' says Williams. 'Please encourage her to get the help – even if you need to get assistance from other resources like relatives or friends to make sure help is there.'

There are many reasons for postnatal depression – and it's vital that you reassure her that's it not a result of her being a bad mother in any way. 'Anyone who has depression will feel like doing a small task is a huge mountain to climb,' adds Williams. The long-term effects of untreated depression like this can devastate families.

CAN DADS GET POSTNATAL DEPRESSION?

Postnatal depression in dads – also called paternal depression – is experienced by around one in 28 new fathers in the first year after the birth of their child, according to data from the Medical Research Council. It can be brought on by emotional and stressful events – like having a baby, and all the side effects of such a life-changing event.

Along with the emotional and psychological disruption – the new responsibility, financial pressures, changes to the way you live your life and in some cases relationship issues with your partner – it can be triggered by the physical demands created by a lack of sleep and a rise in the work-load at home too.

New dads are at a greater risk of depression during the pregnancy, or after their child is born, if there are existing problems in the relationship. Also it's more likely to occur in men if their partner is experiencing depression. Younger dads and those on a low income are especially prone to paternal depression.

WHAT ARE THE SIGNS OF PND IN DADS?

'More men get depressed while dealing with the partner's postnatal depression,' says Mark Williams. 'While the partner is getting treatment, the man may find himself dealing with the illness, work, money issues, household chores and other children.

'After dealing with everything in such a short space of time, the man can become depressed, which can affect the whole family. One of the key factors is to make sure the partner gets the support as well, as they tend to be worse after the partner gets better.

'New fathers who may be suffering will be overwhelmed, feel isolated and can be confused by their feelings and their partner's reaction to them,' says Williams. 'They're often unlikely to play with their newborn, or it may be a big effort to do so. They will lack motivation in themselves, and this can lead to them feeling like a failure. Every father will be different – but some may be moody and aggressive and undergo quite a change of personality.

'Men with postnatal depression can feel trapped and withdrawn – they tend not to open up about their true feelings, so it is important that they seek help with their GP before it could lead to a total breakdown.'

WHAT CAN I DO TO COMBAT PND?

- Talk to your partner, family and friends about how you are feeling.
- Speak to your GP about the methods available for combating depression.

- Realise that it's normal to sometimes feel down or low about being a parent – and try to focus on the plus points and enjoyable moments.
- Stay social – keep in touch with friends and keep yourself in good physical shape. Combine the two by exercising or doing sports with friends.
- Watch out for negative coping strategies – like drinking too much or avoiding going home.

New dads could also get help dealing with their feelings by talking to other new dads or some of the support groups offering advice on coping with parenthood.

Who can help?

There are many good organisations that have support groups and also information on postnatal depression:

Fathers Reaching Out: Network group providing men with help and support to manage and cope with depression in themselves or their partner. www.fathersreachingout.com

MIND: Mental health support group providing counselling and support for sufferers of PND as well as advice for friends or family concerned about the health of a new parent. www.mind.org.uk/0300 123 3393.

PANDAS Foundation: A charity supporting families suffering from pre- (antenatal) and postnatal depression. www.pandasfoundation.org.uk

Association for Post-Natal Illness: Providing support to mothers suffering from postnatal illness. Also aims to increase public awareness of the illness and to encourage research into its cause and nature. www.apni.org

The Smile Group: For those finding parenthood harder than expected, suffering from full-blown postnatal depression or just having a bad day as a new parent. www.thesmilegroup.org

Some dads just find their own ways to deal with the role and the responsibilities it entails. Some fathers will admit in private or public that they're 'reluctant fathers'.

But postnatal depression is something quite different and often intertwined with other challenges in that father's life. It's increasingly being given more attention and recognition, though there remains a stigma regarding all forms of mental illness that make this one especially difficult for some men to confront. The above sensitive support groups provide a service that you can use, anonymously, to get guidance if you feel you need it. Even if it's just dealing with some of the tougher challenges that come with new parenthood.

Wisdom of Fathers

Change Of Life

'I think the hardest thing about becoming a father is actually the general change in life. Because Tanya is breastfeeding we cannot just pop out for a meal or to the cinema. Everything during the day is worked around the three-hour windows between feeds. We have now got him taking expressed milk from a bottle to try to free up some time, but it takes planning again to find the time to express milk between the feeds.' Steve, father of Logan

SHOULD WE HAVE THE BABY IN BED WITH US?

You slaved away creating the ultimate nurturing nursery with a cosy, and possibly quite costly, cot and then – possibly in a fit of sleep-deprived desperation – you or your partner decide to put your baby in bed with you at night.

Sure enough it can be a novel experience as you bond together at bedtime as a family – but, despite the ease of having them sleeping beside you, for many parents it proves to be a hard habit to shake.

Until recently the experts – in the shape of the Royal College of Midwives – would say it has its plus points, especially if it helps with the mother's breastfeeding to have baby in bed with you both. Ideally they'd suggest you only do it if you both agreed on it – avoiding having the baby in with you every night – and certainly never have them in with you if either of you have been drinking or are on any drugs (prescribed or, er, not) that make you feel drowsy.

You'd have to check that there was no way they could fall out, that you've all clipped your toe and finger nails – so as not to accidentally scratch them – and that there's no risk of them suffocating because of very soft pillows or mattresses.

However, new research published in 2013 following studies from the London School of Hygiene and Tropical Medicine suggests that sharing a bed with a newborn increases the risk of sudden infant death syndrome (SIDS) five-fold.

In one estimate around 120 of the 300 cot deaths that occur in the UK each year may be prevented if parents followed guidelines similar to those followed in the USA and the Netherlands. In those countries parents are warned **NOT** to share a bed with their baby for the first three months (12 weeks) of his or her life. And to be as safe as possible the experts suggest that the 'best place for a baby to sleep for the first six months is in a crib or cot in the same room as a parent or carer.'

Wisdom of Fathers

Golden Rules for Good Baby Sleep

Getting a baby to sleep through the night is the subject matter of countless books, magazine features and old wives' tales. If you're finding that the little one doesn't want to get some shut-eye – and is preventing the pair of you from doing it too, try a few tired and testing but successful tricks used by dads in the past:

- 'We made it all part of the routine – change her nappy, put on her bed clothes, have a bedtime story – even when she was way too young to understand them. Seemed to work from the off.' Paul, father of Hannah
- 'Get a night light. We have a soft glow light that allows us to come into the nursery and see okay without putting on the main light and disturbing our baby.' Andy, father of Kyra and George
- 'To make sure Jess didn't get overtired during the day we'd make sure she had plenty of naps then put her down early in the evening for bed, which seemed to work really well, oddly.' Adam, father of Jessica

Wisdom of Fathers

Getting a Baby to Nap

'I'm a stay-at-home dad, I love the role but our daughter was proving to be a real problem when it came to going down for a nap – although she was fine with night-time sleeps. I tried just rocking her in the car seat – I couldn't take her for a drive every time as it would cost me a bundle in fuel. It worked on and off but then someone recommended a vibrating baby chair – battery powered and they just sit in it and it shakes away gently – it was almost hypnotic for Kayla. It helped differentiate the cot for bedtime from the seat for nap time. I used it less and less as she got bigger and now she naps without needing it.' Jamie, father of Kayla

HOW CAN I MAKE SURE MY NEW FAMILY ARE SECURE?

Nothing else quite shows up the change from lad to dad – the end of the feckless carefree days and the start of serious paternal responsibility – than finding yourself having financial advice conversations. Questions like 'what would happen if I weren't around?' or 'how would my new family cope if I were taken seriously ill' aren't exactly fun topics for a Friday night at the bar, but they're ones many new fathers need or now choose to consider.

Dads are worth a great deal – though you may not feel like it sometimes. For starters you're doing more and more housework and childcare than ever before (well, you should be). One survey by an insurance firm estimated that dads do more than £21,000 of work around the house a year, or the equivalent of 50 man hours a week. That's aside from your role as breadwinner. What if – God forbid – you were to have an accident or contract a serious illness, or have this challenging new life as a dad cut short?

The same survey found that a third of new dads admitted to having no life insurance – with over two-thirds having no critical illness cover, which pays out in the event of a serious illness. A few chronically dull but crucially important financial points for new dads to think about would be:

- **Income protection cover:** This is along the lines of under-employment insurance, which pays a regular tax-free income if you can't work because of illness or disability.
- **Life insurance:** Not just Dad but protecting Mum often gets forgotten.
- **Private medical insurance:** If nothing else your recent experiences around your partner's pregnancy and the birth of your child may have you thinking long and hard about the health services on offer to you.
- **Critical illness cover:** The average weekly household expenditure in the UK was estimated at £455 in one survey – but statutory sick pay is only £81.60 per week.
- **Savings for school fees:** Not just university or college fees – the costs of uniforms, books and taking holidays during school holidays can reduce a grown man to tears as his credit card goes into meltdown.

- **Redundancy insurance:** According to the Joseph Rowntree Foundation it costs a couple with two children £29,200 per annum to achieve a basic but acceptable standard of living.
- **The future:** Just providing a sound financial footing for when your baby (which isn't even walking yet) will one day be looking to stand on their own two feet and then step on to the property ladder perhaps.
- **Will/guardianship:** You set out your intentions through a trust or will about who would look after your child or children in the event of both parents dying. After discussing and agreeing it with the relevant prospective guardians of course!

Wisdom of Fathers

Spending Time Together ... And Apart

'Our baby is now four months old, so a lot more active. I enjoy playing with her and reading to her. I wouldn't say the baby has really put a strain on our relationship, but we're both very tired (sometimes stressed) and Baby often sleeps in our bed so no 'TLC' time!

'I'm at work from 8am till 7pm Monday to Thursday (slightly better hours on Friday), so really only get to spend time with our baby on weekends. It's definitely not enough time – I miss her all the time, especially all the little things she's started doing which I miss and my wife has to tell me about. Also, we get lots of visitors on weekends so it sometimes feels like I don't get the chance to even hold my baby.' Sunil, father of Riya at four months

5 NEW LIFE IN THE GREAT OUTDOORS

Child's Life: Weeks 17–20

WHAT'S HAPPENING WITH OUR BABY AT THIS STAGE?

There's no stopping them now. With a healthy dose of breast milk or formula in them and a freshly changed nappy your baby is ready to take on a multitude of challenges at this stage. Be amazed as they:

- Roll themselves into a crawl position on the rug and steady themselves in anticipation of moving ... though they may not quite crawl anywhere just yet.
- Amuse themselves by playing with their own hands and feet – looking at their tootsies as if they're creatures from another planet.
- Respond to sounds, seemingly recognise their own name and even get a bit anxious around strangers.
- Become right little wrigglers – loving nothing more than shuffling along the floor on their belly like a sniper. Parents with wooden floors may want to attach a dusting cloth to their baby's romper suit and get some housework done in the process.
- Try sitting upright at around five months – some babies will hold themselves in place with their hands as they do.

- Waving bye-bye to you – though not necessarily when you're leaving.
- Blowing bubbles – with saliva not a washing-up liquid mixture.

As ever the big disclaimer on this is that all babies are different – some will barely make much of a move right now, others will be rolling around the floor like drunken sailors.

Keep an eye out for some of these behaviours though – and if you really want to earn some brownie points make a note of any landmark movements or developmental milestones in the baby book that you've been recording things in since pregnancy … you did start the baby book, didn't you?

WHAT'S THE BEST WAY TO TAKE OUR BABY OUT AND ABOUT?

Now that the basic baby routines are in place and you're a dab hand at getting out of the house in under an hour, you might start making plans to venture further afield. You might even consider … a holiday. Getting your baby out and about – either in a buggy or a BMW – does necessitate some crucial bits of kit. If you haven't bought yours yet – or you have and you just want to make you weren't ripped off – here's a breakdown of all you'll need and how you can best get it.

PUSHCHAIRS, BUGGIES AND CAR SEATS

Much like buying a new car, when it comes to the 'chariot' to take baby from A to B – via Starbucks for a quick nappy change – there's a baby buggy to fit every financial profile, every taste, every lifestyle and every desire to outdo the person next to you in the queue at Mothercare.

The modern buggy has advanced to dovetail nicely into your lifestyle – way beyond simply being easy to park in the coffee shop. Outdoor pursuit dads may want to take a long hard look – with no small amount of tyre-kicking and 'spec' reading – at the pushchairs that will enable you to bound along with baby. See www.mountainbuggy.com

Three-in-one and two-in-one pushchairs/prams

Shaped like a pram but able to convert into a pushchair that faces forward or rearward, these range from sturdy and reliable, like the Graco Symbio 3-1 at £230, up to the fashionable head-turning Bugaboo Cameleon 3 at £830. (Look for ones that feature a Group 0 car seat, rain cover and parasol.)

Travel systems

These are similar to the 3-in-1 models and also feature a removable car seat that doubles as a carrier for shipping your kid around the home too. There is also a pushchair chassis and basket for carrying spares (accessories not spare babies). Example: Graco Quattro Tour Sport Travel System at £299.99.

All-terrain pushchairs/'three-wheelers'

Certainly less likely to tumble over than the *Only Fools and Horses* three-wheeler, these are built for rocky roads, country life or council-pothole-negligence urban living. They have rubber types to stop your baby feeling every peak and trough on the path ahead. They're also made to be as light as possible – be prepared for some swearing trying to wrestle it on to a bus though. They are not cheap, but built to last. For example the Quinny Buzz 3 at £364.99.

Folding pushchairs

With a forward-facing design and storage basket underneath, these are especially easy to fold and very lightweight, so ideal for parents using public transport a lot. They are usually aimed at the older child – something to downsize to once your child is toddling especially. Market leaders include Maclaren, whose Techno XT at £185 is a nippy little runabout in this category.

Take a look online at the great variety of chariots available to new parents and check out the tips below before buying.

Bugaboo, www.bugaboo.com
Chicco, www.chicco.co.uk
Graco, www.graco.co.uk
Maclaren, www.maclarenbaby.com
Mothercare, www.mothercare.com
Quinny, www.quinny.com

Dad You Know?

Relax When They're Facing You

Recent research from the University of Dundee shows that babies who are pushed in prams or buggies that face towards the parent rather than away from them are less stressed. Dads are also twice as likely to speak to their baby when they're in a buggy facing them – and the researchers found that facing their fathers made babies more likely to laugh and more self-aware.

WHAT DO I NEED TO KNOW WHEN BUYING THE 'CHARIOT'?

Familiarise yourself with the line – often snarled through gritted teeth – that goes something like: 'there's a knack to doing this'. It's common parlance among frustrated new fathers and bewildered pushchair salesmen alike as they attempt to fold down or set up a new buggy. Don't be surprised to find yourself part of a 'tag team' attempting to carry out this simple task.

To take the stress out of pushchair management remember some of the following rules, gleaned from first-time fathers who've experienced this ride before:

- **Practice erection and collapse:** What works in the shop with the assistant on hand won't be half as easy when you or your partner are alone, trying to 'bring down' a buggy while possibly clutching your offspring in your other hand. Make sure you're both confident with setting up a collapsible buggy by yourself. If necessary, take the unusual step of consulting the manual.

- **Shake it in your booty:** Take measurements of the push-chair including its depth when folded down to ensure you can fit it in your car – and when it's upright to make sure it'll squeeze through your front door too.

- **Look for offers:** One new father tipped me off that Mothercare offer an online discount code for 10 per cent, which he used to get down the cost of a new Bugaboo buggy. 'It seems to change every year but if you search round the blogs you can find it.' Aside from the street cred of this particular model the same dad said it was the kind of buggy that comes with detachable fabric that you throw in to the washing machine as and when you need to. 'Which helps with its sell-on value too.'

- **Try, say bye, then buy:** Try out one of the pushchairs or buggies at the department store. Get the full spec details and don't be afraid to ask questions. Then go look online and see if you're able to find it for less somewhere else.

- **Don't be overwhelmed:** Put together a checklist of what you're going to really need. Does a system that offers a car seat have much worth if neither of you drive? Will you or your partner need to use public transport a lot? What's the terrain like around your home?

Dad You Know?

Back Problems with Buggies

What works for others may not work for you. Indeed the height and handle position that your partner pushes your baby at may need to be adjusted when you use it. Look for one that you can tailor in this way – and, although online buying is a great option, do try to test-drive any buggy in the store before buying (ideally with it adjusted to a height you're both comfortable with).

Dads, you may need to check that there is sufficient distance between your step as you walk and the back axles of the buggy – ensure it can accommodate your natural stride. According to a survey by BackCare – the charity for healthier backs – poor pushchair-pushing posture not only makes for a great tongue twister but also accounts for back pain in an estimated 73 per cent of new parents.

DOES OUR BABY NEED A CAR SEAT YET?

Yep, if you're taking your baby anywhere by car then the law – and common sense for that matter – says that they need to be secure in a seat that's securely fastened to the rigid chunky bits within the adult car seats. (The law in the UK dictates that kids today must use some form of car seat or booster from the age of 0 up to the age of 12.)

A range of high-street retailers sell the most popular car seats, and it's best to buy new from someone who knows what they're talking about. One survey by *Mother & Baby* magazine found that as many as 80 per cent of child car seats are not properly fitted. In another study – carried out by Which? – car experts visited the Bluewater shopping centre and offered parents a free car seat inspection. Just two of the 27 seats inspected were fitted correctly. The leading brands to look at when drawing up your budget include:

Bébé Confort, www.bebeconfort.com
Britax, www.britax.co.uk
Graco, www.graco.co.uk
Maxi-Cosi, www.maxi-cosi.co.uk
Mamas and Papas, www.mamasandpapas.com

WHAT AM I LOOKING FOR WHEN BUYING THE BABY'S CAR SEAT?

As tempting as it is in these cash-strapped times to go second-hand on these more pricey purchases – it's advisable that you don't skimp on the car seat. The Royal Society for the Prevention of Accidents (RoSPA) is just one of the organisations that advise parents against buying second-hand car seats or sourcing them from car-boot sales and the like, just in case there's a hidden fault with the seat or it may have been damaged in an accident.

Since your baby's safety is at stake it's worth erring on the side of caution on this one and even refusing the offer of a free seat from an old friend whose kid has grown out of theirs.

For babies you need to go for the rear-facing Group 0 (that's the size) car seat. This should keep your kid safe and sound from birth up until 9–12 months – or when they weigh up to 9 kg (20 lbs). When they're bigger, heavier and able to sit up unaided and support their head on their own you may well want to look at super-sizing your car seat.

Next is the group 0+, which can adjust, so that it'll take a baby from birth up to 13 kg (29 lb), which is around 12–15 months. If you're after something that would last longer then models such as the Britax First Class are suitable from birth–four years (birth–18 kg/40 lb). It can be used rearward facing up to 13 kg and then switches to forward facing for 9–18 kg (20–40 lb).

Why don't I just buy the 0–4 year one?

Good question. Answers include: because they're pricier. Because you may change car or have more kids or both. Also because your baby will eat, sleep, dribble, poo, wee and generally 'live' in this seat at times. Imagine how it's going to be looking by the fourth year in this case?

Will the seat fit my car?

If your car was manufactured after 1999 it should come with ISOFIX (International Standards Organisation Fix) anchors either side of the cushion in the rear passenger seat. These are the clumpy, lumpy rigid bolts that are welded to the chassis of the car. They offer more security for the seat than alternatives – such as threading an adult seat belt through plastic slots, as some car seats offer.

The position of these anchorage points can vary between different models of cars. As a result it's pretty tough trying to find a seat that fits all cars, and, while the ISOFIX points are designed to get around this, some models of car only take some types of ISOFIX seat. To see which seat will fit your car, check your car manufacturer's website – compatible models should be listed. Alternately speak to the specialists at the store you're buying a seat from – Halfords do have dedicated car-seat people on hand to run you through the types of car seats available and to help you fit them securely.

If you're going to be driving with your child pretty regularly throughout its first year or so – possibly dropping them with baby minders – then be sure to check out the seats that come with separate base models.

With this type the base clips into the car's ISOFIX points – then the seat itself secures into the base. They're just as safe – but once fitted you don't have to be remove the whole seat frame every time you take your baby out of the car. You simply click the seat back into place for each journey.

HOW CAN YOU FIT A BABY CAR SEAT THE WRONG WAY?

The devil is in the detail here with the tiniest of mis-fittings potentially having catastrophic consequences. Among some of the common errors that dads and mums had committed when taking their baby on the road were:

Twisted seat belts

Check that the seat belt has no kinks or twists in it that could stop it from reacting as it should in the event of the car being in a collision. Just give it a couple of 'pings' whenever you put your child in the chair to see that the belt's running smoothly and securely through any fittings.

Loose seat belts and harnesses

In the rush to hit the road it's possible that the fasteners aren't clicked into place properly and secured tightly. Take a second to undo them and fasten them again just to be doubly sure.

Buckle crunch

Positioning the car's seat belt buckle hard up against the child seat frame can cause the buckle to fail under crash conditions. Try to make sure that only the seat belt webbing comes into contact with the frame of the car seat. If the buckle of the adult belt lies across the frame of the child seat, pressure on the buckle (in an accident, or even under sharp braking) could cause the buckle to fail – leading to your baby being unrestrained and possibly coming out of their seat.

Dad You Know?

Get the Car Seat You Asked For ...

Research conducted by iCarhireinsurance revealed that 12 per cent of customers renting a car have expressed concern over the safety of their child due to the condition of their car seat. The same study showed that 37 per cent of rental car users were left to their own devices when it came to installing a child seat in their rented car. If you're going to be hiring a child seat with your car – sometimes the cost is on a par with buying the bleeding thing outright – insist on getting the following in return:

Before you book your vehicle ask about their child-seat policy and ask what you can expect to receive.

Do your research, get online and look for reviews from other families.

Ask if you will receive assistance with your car seat or instructions, and plan ahead if you think you might arrive out of the company's rental hours.

It is always best to be prepared for the worst – consider packing a thin blanket to cover the child seat in the event that it is dirty.

TRAVEL

HOW CAN I ENSURE WE ALL ENJOY OUR TIME IN THE CAR?

Imagine you're stuck in a barely-moving four-mile tailback and you're not likely to be gearing up for a long time yet. Now think of all the ways to keep your just-out-of-reach child happy – it will be worth it:

- Your baby son or daughter's first 'optional extra' could be a car sun shade. (Yes, even in this country you may have days when you need to shade your baby from the glare of the sun through a glass windscreen.) You can get smiley face or cartoon character shades that stick on the windscreen. Or if you're already seething at having to deface your motor with a 'Baby On Board' sticker then opt for the roller-blind type.
- Fit the baby's seat so he or she is sat behind the driver – that way the adult in the passenger seat can easily turn around to check on them from the front.
- Fit a mini mirror that sticks to the inside of your rear windscreen. Angle it so you can see your baby in this mirror when you look into your rear-view mirror.
- If the fittings allow, put a plastic sheet under the case seat or base to keep any food, milk, crumbs and much worse off the upholstery.
- Re-stock the glove compartment with wipes, cloths and an air freshener ... especially an air freshener.
- Get into the habit of keeping a kid's bag in the boot – stocked with toys, books and a spare blanket.
- Once your kid is old enough for a forward-facing seat – also fit a protective cover to the back of your seat. Muddy wellies won't do the upholstery any favours.

Weird Things Babies Do

Driven to Distraction

A quarter of all new dads have driven their babies on average up to 30 miles a week in the car to settle them to sleep.

WHY SHOULD I TAKE MY BABY OUT IN A CARRIER?

You may have already got in to the habit of taking your baby out as a proud new dad at every opportunity, but if you haven't, or you're just keen to discover new ways of bonding with them, then the baby carrier could be the way forward.

Although more baby carriers are sold as 'ready to use from birth' – it's only as your baby's back and neck muscles are sufficiently developed for them to hold their head up that you can start to carry your baby facing forward – and show them the world.*

Don't just strap them on to your chest and strut outside though. Engage in some mind-stimulating activity (for both baby and you) while you're wearing them in the carrier – by doing so you can start laying the foundations for their learning too:

- Point out things when you're walking – bus, dog, park, etc. and say the words out loud.
- Hold up books or newspapers you're looking at when you've got them in their carrier.
- Chat with other parents doing the same thing and allow the babies to interact too.

MEDICAL ADVICE:

During the very first months, however, you should NOT carry your child facing forward at all, as the child's neck muscles are not sufficiently developed to support his/her head.

* Take note, some spiteful types will mock the modern father who wears his kid with pride in the way. Some proud dads who present their offspring in these papoose-like arrangements have been accused of showing off their virility or using their babe as a magnet for, well, babes.

The benefits of taking your baby out and about in a carrier are that you're able to walk around and not have to struggle negotiating steps or buses with your baby in a buggy or pushchair. So long as you follow the strap-on instructions it's a safe and fun way to experience their new world, while leaving your hands free to do important stuff like online betting, Facebook status updates, etc.

One study – admittedly it was by baby product firm Johnson's – even suggested that babies suffer from a form of sensory deprivation in the Western, modernised world we're in because they spend so long in car seats or prams – and no longer have the primitive interaction with parents that come with being carried by mum and dad.

Either way it's pretty useful to put your kid in a carrier sometimes rather than have to wrestle up flights of stairs or on to buses with a Bugaboo. Just don't leave your baby dangling in its carrier for too long for the sake of their spine – and yours!

WHAT DO I NEED TO TAKE WITH ME ... ASIDE FROM THE BABY?

Babies love nothing more than to observe their surroundings with their back nestling safely against Mum or Dad.* These days the harnesses are available in a range of designs and colours including sleek black ones and shades that'll match your favourite football team shirt.

Before you buy one though, take a moment to check it's fully fitted for papoose-like purpose:

- Remember the safety rules about carrying new babies and ensure your carrier supports them fully. There's an increasingly wide variety of brands, from the traditional Scandiwegian purveyors of kiddie carrier – BabyBjörn

---

* Actually no one knows what they love more of at this age, but it's a fairly good guess that being carried around and shown the sights, stopping only to have some snack or your bum wiped is a fairly fun position to be in.

through to the Tomy Freestyle Classic Carrier or a Tippitoes 2 Way Front Baby Carrier. Any one with a BS EN 13209 Part 2:2005 safety mark is recommended.

- Try it for size – and more crucially try to work out how to fit the blasted thing. Carriers like the BabyBjörn range feature some 'rigging' that needs to be adjusted to fit you and baby comfortably so it'll pay to have a few practice runs beforehand.
- Get used to standing, sitting and manoeuvring with baby *in situ* – before you have the mandatory 'first outing with Daddy' photo taken.
- Don't forget your dad bag. You may want to try to match this up to your baby carrier if you're especially fashion-conscious. Either way, a man bag, backpack or LP-carrier style that contains the following is a must for every modern father:
  - Changing mat – with a wipe-down and fold-away surface for comfort and cleanliness during the removal of kid's cack.

Wisdom of Fathers

Baby Traits

'At four months Nellie started waking up in a good mood with cooing and smiling rather than screaming for a bottle. She's also started sleeping through the night (well, five hours at a time). From a physical perspective, she has started to roll on to her side, is reaching for things and is practising grabbing things, has just started teething and is smiling and giggling at some things. New sounds are appearing such as "gwig gwig" and "gwag gwag", and she actively engages with everyone. She has one noticeable trait, which is holding one arm up in the air for an extended period of time, which we theorise is either some rallying technique to unite babies of the world or receiving instructions from her overlord beings.' Chris, father of Nellie, Meredith and Milly

- Baby wipes and disposal bag (a must).
- Nappies (don't leave home without them).
- Baby formula/milk, bottles and bib.
- Sun hat and sunscreen (at least SPF 50 or complete sunblock) for the baby, though you must keep your baby out of direct exposure to the sun completely – especially since their skin will be very sensitive and could react badly to the sun cream.
- Woolly hat, additional blankets and extra layers for cold weather trips. A snuggle cover is also good because babies can't generate heat in the way that adults can. Cover them up when outdoors in the cold.

OVERSEAS TRAVEL

WHEN CAN WE TAKE OUR BABY OVERSEAS?

Many airlines like you to wait at least 48 hours after the baby is born before flying with them, while medical advice usually advocates taking them after they've had the preliminary baby vaccinations at the very least. Talk to your GP or travel clinic or contact the Health Protection Agency (www.hpa.org.uk) for the latest up-to-date information on additional medical protection your baby may need.

Whether you're going abroad to show off your new baby to distant friends or relatives – or just taking a well-earned break – the task of taking a baby under two with you adds a whole new level of stress to what's often already a traumatising event. But with a bit of pre-planning you can make taking Baby on board a lot easier.

DO I NEED A PASSPORT FOR A BABY?

Yep, your baby will need a passport to travel abroad. It will be valid for five years, even though by the time it needs updating they'll look nothing like the photo inside.

It can be applied for from your local post office – or you can apply for a form online (www.postoffice.co.uk). You'll need two identical colour pics of your nipper (see photo tips in Chapter 11) – one of these needs to be signed on the back by a professional (someone from a respectable occupation such as teacher, GP, solicitor and, er, journalist, oddly) who's known you (for two years) and your baby.

You'll need your baby's birth certificate and proof of your nationality – plus a payment of £49.00. (You read that right.)

HOW EASY IS IT TO TAKE A BABY ON A PLANE?

So long as it isn't someone else's baby you'll be able to travel by plane with pretty much the same level of hassle, aggravation and stress as you would without a child in tow. There are even some priorities given to parents when it comes to boarding, and many airports have facilities for baby changing and breastfeeding. But just to make things a little bit awkward, different airlines have different rules about carrying babies – and more specifically about carrying quantities of baby's milk – so it's worth checking out the specifics of the carrier you're flying with well in advance.

A few useful pointers that British Airways provided me with may come in useful for you too if you're heading overseas, especially on a long haul.

- Airlines do offer discounts for little ones but they vary – depending on the airline and where your infant sits. BA, for example, offer an infant fare – at 10 per cent of the adult fare – if the infant sits on an adult's lap for the whole flight. Not so bad for Heathrow to Edinburgh – far from fun for the London to Auckland ride.
- Once your child is two years of age or older they HAVE to sit in their own seat.

Does the baby get an in-flight meal?

'Some airlines carry some tinned baby food on our long-haul flights,' explains Edith Garrard, a 'Flying Auntie' with British Airways. 'But we recommend you carry your own baby food and equipment, including liquids and sterilised bottles, in your hand baggage. With BA you can bring baby milk with you and there is no "100 ml of liquid" rule – but be aware this rule may differ abroad. If you'd like to bring your own baby food with you, make sure you bring unopened food in a sealed jar.'

Airport security regulations may be different from one terminal to another. If you can, check what restrictions are in place in the airports you're travelling to, from and via. Also don't rely on the air crew being able to sterilise any bottles on board.

You may be able to reserve a seat facing a bulkhead that has a carrycot position – enabling you to put them in a cot on a fold-down support – on some airlines. British Airways will provide carrycots if booked in advance. When you fly with your baby on your lap you're given an extension seat belt. This clips to your own and holds them in place securely whenever that little belt light above your head tells you to clip them in.

Infants are allowed one checked bag except on hand-baggage-only fares. If you're driving and parking at the departure airport then you can often book parking in advance, which is cheaper, and use family parking bays if you're travelling with children, which takes some of the aggro out of the journey. 'You can bring a small folding pushchair and car seat if needed (the car seat will go in the hold as luggage). You can use the pushchair up to the point of boarding your flight, after which the cabin crew will put it in the hold,' says Garrard.

If you can, try to book flights that coincide with your baby's sleep pattern so they're less likely to be disturbed by all that's going on – and nor will those sat around you.

WHAT DO WE NEED WHEN GOING OUT IN THE SUN?

Whether you're holidaying overseas or enjoying a rare moment of sunshine in the UK, you need to be especially on guard against the effects of the sun on Baby's skin.

Because your baby's skin is so sensitive, parents are advised to keep their baby out of direct sunlight through the first six months of their lives – and even after that it's best to keep them in the shade whenever possible.

When you're taking your baby out on a sunny day be sure to protect them with a hat and a sun shade or parasol that'll fix to their buggy.

Be sure to slather sunscreen on the areas of their skin that aren't covered by their clothes – you can also use zinc oxide on Baby's nose, ears and lips, which offers some great potential for comedy photos. Use gentle formula sun creams – with SPF 50 – and reapply every hour or as instructed to do so. (E.g. Johnson's SunCare Baby SPF 50 sun protection cream, 50ml, £8.99.)

Baby sunglasses (e.g. Baby Banz, £12, age 0–2 years) don't just look cute – they also do protect children's eyes from harmful rays.

If they do suffer mild sunburn apply a cool cloth to their skin for 10–15 minutes a few times daily – for more severe sunburn, take them to the GP immediately. Watch out for 'prickly heat' too – a rash that infants' skin is especially prone to. It appears as small pink-red bumps on the areas where your baby sweats – skin folds, armpits and around the nappy fittings.

WHAT SHOULD I DO IF OUR BABY GETS INSECT BITES OR STINGS?

Just because they're wrapped in a blanket, snuggled inside a pram and surrounded by love your baby isn't immune to the odd bite or sting from the various beasts that plague the nation's parks and beer gardens.

The key concern to look out for is a possible allergic reaction to a bite or sting – something you won't really know about with your baby until it happens. If you notice a shortness of breath in your baby after you suspect they've been stung, call 999 immediately.

In the main the worst thing to happen when your baby is stung is just that, a sting. Bees can sometimes leave their sting behind in the skin so you should remove that without squeezing the sac containing the venom that may still be attached to the barb. You can try to flick this out with a credit card – if you only carry cash then tweezers are the ideal tool for this particular job.

CHILDCARE

HOW DO WE GET CHILDCARE – AND WHAT WILL IT COST US?

Round about now, the end of your partner's maternity leave is probably on the horizon and you'll have to make big decisions about how to make life work at that point. One of the biggest concerns for today's parents is the rising cost of childcare. So many factors need to be weighed up when you're looking at ways of juggling work and childcare, especially in their pre-school years.

Some families are able to call in the aid of their own parents or extended family to help out, but for more and more new mums and dads it's a case of going out to work and spending a significant amount of what you bring home to pay someone else to look after your child.

What you pay for childcare will vary according to factors such as where you live, the age of your child and the type and duration of childcare you're after. You may have an employer who provides subsidised childcare arrangements – you can find out more about the specifics of how these work via support groups like the Family and Childcare Trust (www.daycaretrust. org.uk) and Working Families (www.workingfamilies.org.uk). They're also really useful to help you work out if you're eligible for financial help in your childcare provision through things like working tax credits and childcare vouchers.

WHAT ARE THE DIFFERENT TYPES OF CHILDCARE?

The cost of professional, secure child provision isn't cheap – but then would you want it to be? If one or both of you are working full- or part-time you're going to need to sit down and discuss how best to schedule your time, arrange pick-up and drop-off times possibly and work out your finances to ensure your little one has the best of care while you also get to be with them as much as you can too.

According to a 2013 survey by online childcare search site www.findababysitter.com, shopping around for the right provision can save you up to £2,000 a year. Here are some of the options available to new parents and the kinds of costs involved.

Full-time day nursery

Daycare nurseries offer full daycare for babies as young as three months up to school-aged children. Typically, costs per child per week run from £160–200 depending on whereabouts in the country you're looking. As babies and toddlers need hands-on care and one-to-one attention, nurseries use more staff and may well charge penalties for late collection of children.

To find out more about day nurseries, contact the National Day Nurseries Association: www.ndna.org.uk. Your local authority should also have contact details for registered, and therefore Ofsted-inspected, nurseries.

Mind that child!

Registered childminders look after one or more children under the age of eight for more than a total of two hours a day – says the Professional Association for Childcare and Early Years (www.pacey.org.uk). They usually do this from their own home and are self-employed – and, while costs vary from area to area, the www.findababysitter.com survey found that an average cost of £6.61 per hour was the going rate (from a study of 170,000 registered childcare professionals). Registered childminders are inspected by Ofsted in England (or the Care and Social Services Inspectorate – CSSIW – in Wales). These checks ensure they provide a safe and stimulating environment for the kids. Childminders are responsible for providing meals and snacks for the children and arranging fun and learning activities for them.

Grab a nanny

Often the most expensive childcare option – the www.findababysitter.com survey found that nanny costs average around £8.60 per hour. Employing a full-time nanny also means you'll be responsible for employer duties such as a contract and paying tax and national insurance for them. You can find Ofsted-registered nannies at sources such as www.childcare.co.uk, www.nationalnannies.co.uk or local and national agencies. Some nannies will live in – again their salary will vary according to your locale. You may have a part-time nanny or even one whose role includes housekeeper too.

'Ave an au pair

From the French term meaning 'on a par with', an au pair is seen as being equal to a member of the family that they will usually be living with. Often employed via agencies, au pairs are often at the student stage of childcare – learning their craft – and many come to the UK from overseas to work and in doing so learn about British culture and the English language too. If they're living in your family home you will need to cover the additional expenses that come with having another adult around the house – but the au pair is often viewed as being at the more affordable end of childcare options since their rates are considerably lower than qualified nannies or established nurseries.

Calling in family favours

Having your child's grandparents or other close relatives or friends help out with childcare does have its benefits. You'll know them (obviously) and will be able to agree on issues such as payment or covering expenses (hopefully). But it can come with its difficulties too – especially if there's a conflict between you or your partner and the carer about such issues as how your baby is raised or what kind of hours they're expected to put in. Try to review the situation regularly, avoid taking them for granted and allow them to have their own time off.

Dad You Know?

Nanny Mc Fees

The costliest nurseries are more expensive than top public schools – a place at Britain's most expensive nursery this year (£42,000) costs 30 per cent more than a place at a top public school such as Charterhouse (£30,574 per year).

(Daycare Trust and Family and Parenting Institute survey, 2013)

HOW DO WE KNOW OUR CHILDCARE IS SAFE FOR OUR BABY?

Parents should check that childminders are Ofsted-registered. Ofsted require that childminders undergo training including first-aid care and are subject to a current CRB (Criminal Records Bureau) check – this is undergoing a change to a DBS (Disclosure and Barring Service).

Ofsted inspections are carried out every three years. You can find a report of your childminder's most recent inspection via www.ofsted.gov.uk. Some childminders are listed by name – others by their unique reference number, which will be on their Ofsted certificate and begin with the prefix EY (Early Years).

Wisdom of Fathers

Au Pair Care with Benefits

'If you're got a spare room and your finances can allow it I'd get an au pair to do the childcare. We have a girl from Spain who works five days a week looking after our now three-year-old daughter – it gives us much more flexibility, we have a live-in babysitter too, and the fact that she's Spanish means my daughter has learnt to speak another language, which has been an awesome gift for our little girl too.' Tom, father to Coco at three years

WHAT DOES A GOOD NURSERY LOOK LIKE?

It's well worth taking the time to look around the facilities at the nursery or children's centre you're taking your baby along to. It pays to talk to parents who already use it to get their input and take advantage of any open days they could offer for you to try them out. Don't work solely on cost – though that's likely to be an influencing factor for sure. Try to get a feel for what's on offer and talk to the staff there and ask questions about:

- Its location, security, the safety of the neighbourhood and the streets around it.
- The building's maintenance – who looks after it, is it in need of modernisation or repair?
- Are there outdoor play areas – that are also sheltered from the sun?
- How many staff are there? What's the rate of staff turnover? What's the ratio of children to a carer? In England, by law it should be 3:1 for children one and under, and 4:1 for two year olds.
- What are the staff qualifications – are they all trained to supervise your child?

- What food and drinks do they get – do you have to provide them? How will they meet any specific dietary requirements your baby has?
- What's the procedure for collecting and dropping off your baby? What should happen if you're not going to be there at your allotted time?
- What is the centre policy regarding children with infectious illnesses – and you may want to ask about behaviour and discipline, TV watching and nap-time procedures for older children too.

HOW DO I FIND A BABYSITTER?

Time away from your baby – like the odd 'date night' out – can help keep your relationship strong and give you both a much-needed break, even if it's just for a few hours.

But for many young families with no close relatives it can be tough finding someone to look after your little one. You may not want to put upon friends or may not know many people if you're new to an area. You may simply just want someone who does babysitting regularly and has all the right credentials.

Seeking them out

Babysitters offer their services online, via agencies, in adverts in newsagents' windows, at children's centres and through parenting and childcare websites, or you may be recommended one by a friend.

Interviewing them

'Whether it's a full-time nanny or part-time babysitter, have a clear description of the job for them,' says Tom Harrow, director of www.findababysitter.com. In the case of a babysitter, find out who they've sat for before, the ages of the children they looked after and talk to their 'references' too.

Briefing them

Tell the babysitter about your baby's routine, what they're eating and when, and any specific medical needs or house rules – e.g. 'don't allow the cat in the bedroom'. Let them know what's expected of them – no drinking alcohol, no inviting friends around – with regards to how things are done in your home. Provide some food for them and offer to hire a DVD or rent a film of their choice to pass the time if they want.

Arming them ...

... with contact phone numbers for both you and your partner – so in the unlikely event of an emergency they can call you. Let them know where you're heading out to and what time you expect to be home. 'Along with the agreed pay rate you should also arrange a lift home or a taxi for your babysitter if they're going to be leaving your home when it's dark,' says Harrow.

CAN I CLAIM BACK CHILDCARE COSTS?

From 2015 an estimated 2.5 million working families may be able to claim back up to £1,200 in childcare costs as part of a new government scheme set to take effect.

Parents will be allowed to claim back 20 per cent of a total of around £6,000 – a government estimate of the average annual price of a childcare nursery place. The scheme will involve parents opening an online nursery voucher account, in which, for every 80p parents pay into the account, the government adds 20p. The parents then use the vouchers to pay for Ofsted-regulated childcare. In August 2013 the government announced plans to extend the scheme to cover carers taking maternity or paternity leave. The initial proposal is that parents earning up to £150,000 per year – each – could qualify when it's launched.

HOW DO WE GET OUR SEX LIFE BACK?

What's that I hear you say? 'He's banging on about sex again – didn't we have enough in Chapter 3?' Well, such are the complexities of the postnatal relationship that – while sex often is back on the menu within a couple of months of the birth – don't be wholly surprised if it still isn't on for a while yet.

While the physical healing process shouldn't necessarily be an issue for your partner it may still be – especially after a traumatic birth – as can tiredness, feelings of low self-esteem and just a lack of desire bought on by the demands of parenthood.

While you and she may be sharing some intimate moments, it can take time for your sex life to get back to the way it was – in terms of frequency and the sense of enjoyment you get from it. In a study in the *British Journal of General Practice* of 78 first-time mothers only 30 per cent ranked their sex life as 'good' – and that was EIGHT months after giving birth.

But if you're looking to nudge things along a little, here's what a sex expert suggests new dads should do:

Dad You Know?

Rucking Hell

The number of arguments that couples have in the first year of parenthood increases by 40 per cent when compared to pre-baby rows. In a survey of new mums and dads two-thirds of the 3,000 parents polled admitted that these are – in hindsight – often silly arguments that are caused or exacerbated by stress and exhaustion. The most common causes of arguments are whose turn it is to change nappies (33 per cent) and do the night feeds (24 per cent). One in five of the parents polled said they did not receive enough attention from their partner after the birth of their baby.

Buy her a wig

'Okay, maybe you don't have to go that far, but if you can get her to feel different it might help kick-start her sexual desire,' says Siski Green, author of *How To Blow Her Mind In Bed*. 'The problem is that being a "hot sexy mama" is actually really difficult. Even if she was the kind of woman who'd spout filthy come-ons during sex before you had your baby, it's likely that now she feels a tad out of touch with that side of herself.'

'Letting her take on a new persona by getting geared up in fancy dress costumes, wearing a wig, or even just taking her out of her usual environment to a couples-only hotel or similar, will help her shake off her "mama bear head" and get back into sex kitten mode.'

Clear the decks

'There was a time – when having sex – where the thought that people might see or hear you seemed thrilling and sexy,' says Green. 'It heightened the tension, made you both work faster and felt pretty exciting.' Now, the thought of your child waking up or when they're a little older even walking into the bedroom, doesn't make it feel exciting, it makes you both nervous. 'How can she relax enough to get aroused or reach orgasm when every time you grunt she thinks it's the baby calling from the cot? So have the baby stay over at your parents or book a babysitter and go to a hotel, whatever it takes to give her a clear mind so she focuses completely on you and sex.'

Earn it

'No matter how much housework you do your wife isn't going to have sex with you unless she wants to – but she's more likely to want to if you do the dishes, put a wash on, fold some laundry or just take the baby out for an hour,' suggests Green. There are two reasons this works:

1 The more time she has to look after herself, to relax, to simply stop and breathe for a moment, the more spare energy, time and desire she has for sex.
2 She feels loved. If you hire someone to do all that stuff for her, she'll have more time but nothing says 'I care' as much as doing these things yourself.

Inject passion

'Kiss her with passion every day,' says Green. 'One of the main problems with trying to have sex with someone who's not really into it is that every time you go in for your approach, she senses that you're after sex and it immediately makes her want to back off.'

'It's because she kind of wants to do it in her own time in her own way. So rather than trying to get her into bed, keep showing her that your passion is on-going but in a way that doesn't make her feel she has to turn you down. Kisses are ideal for this.'

When you leave for work or wherever, kiss her on the lips for longer than usual, and hook her waist with your arm, bringing her body close to yours. 'Then leave. Do this often. It tells her you're still sexually attracted to her but that you're not expecting every passionate kiss to lead to sex. That leaves the door wide open for her to show you when she's ready to take things further.'

HOW DO WE KEEP OUR RELATIONSHIP STRONG FOR OUR BABY'S SAKE?

Raising a baby isn't all fun and games. In fact for a lot of couples the strain of the job can cause problems in a previously harmonious relationship or widen any cracks that had occurred before Baby came along. Without a close support network of friends or family new parents can struggle to find the time or help to solve any issues that are causing conflict in the relationship. Don't feel you're alone in this. Most new parents experience stress, and often those closest to us can come into the firing line. There are support groups who will help you overcome problems. These include:

Relate (www.relate.org.uk): The country's largest provider of relationship support, with services that include relationship counselling for individuals and couples, family counselling, counselling for children and young people, and sex therapy.

Family Matters Institute (www.familymatters.org.uk): A group of charities and church support networks focused on fatherhood, parenting and marriage and couple relationships, including family breakdown.

National Family Mediation (www.NFM.org.uk): A voluntary-sector provider of family mediation – it's an umbrella organisation of charities offering family mediation and supporting provision to those going through the process of family breakdown, with the motto: 'helping separated parents stay close to their children.'

A TIME OF TEETHING AND WEANING

Child's Life: Weeks 21–24

WHAT'S HAPPENING WITH OUR BABY AT THIS STAGE?

Maybe it was last month, maybe it'll be next month, but at some point around now your baby will be wriggling or crawling or sitting up and tipping over. They may not seem like landmark events and aren't really great statements of child development to boast about against other competitive dads, but they're monumental to your baby in their own way. It means they've joined an independence movement. (Well, they're becoming a tad more independent and they're getting a clumsy hang of the whole movement thing.) Other stuff that could be happening around now is:

- They're able to distinguish between bold colours. This won't influence their dress sense but you'll notice it more now you've read this, I bet.
- They'll be attracted by the shimmering reflection of light on water too – making trips to the swimming pool even more of a wild time for them.
- They could be hauling themselves into the crawling position – steadying themselves like a newborn foal but not actually going anywhere.

- They may have added rolling in different directions to their repertoire.
- They put pretty much anything that isn't bolted down into their mouth.
- They point at things they want, point at things they don't want and leave you to figure it out.
- Pulling hair could be getting an early run-out around this time too.

WHAT ROUTINE CHANGES ARE OCCURRING AT SIX MONTHS?

More growth, more change. Of course each routine is different for each baby but if you put me on the spot I'd hazard a guess at a routine for a six-month-old baby looking a lot like this:

07:00 – Wake and wriggle around the cot until you or Mum shows up. Nappy change for the first time in 12 hours possibly ... good luck with that.

07:15 – Full English breast or solids followed by washing and dressing.

07:30–10:30 – Morning activities, play, walk out in the buggy.

10:30 – Nappy change and a morning nap

11:30 – Wake up and snack time. Play and engage time.

13:00 – Lunch time! Solids and bottle or breast combo!

13:30 – Nap time.

15:00 – Wake up and snack before play indoors or out for a walk.

17:30 – Din-dins! Solids should be on the menu by now.

18:00 – Bathtime and play with some reading too before final bottle feed of the day.

19:30 – Bedtime.

WHAT SHOULD I BE DOING AT THIS STAGE?

You won't need any of those pictures taken with your phone to tell you that a baby at six months old is a whole lot different to one at six weeks old. Not only is this a handy time to re-assess your baby's routine, but as they become more active and their needs and habits change so you may want to look at your own set-up too.

With changes to their feeding behaviour you may want to get more involved in food preparation – allowing your partner more time to focus on other aspects of motherhood ... like catching up on six months of lost sleep.

Your baby will be less dependent on your partner for food now – even if she's still breastfeeding, weaning on to solid foods around now means that you'll be playing a more active role in feeding them. They may even be making initial forays into feeding themselves.

Their sleep patterns may have changed and what worked for you both a few months back – in terms of who does what in the night – may need to change too. Your baby will be sleeping less during the day and engaging more. They'll be increasingly active – which in its own way creates a whole new set of factors to consider. Aside from 'baby-proofing' the home, you may want to start taking them out more.

Calling it a 'review stage' makes it sound like something akin to death by PowerPoint, but you may find that around this time you can re-think how the pair of you look after your baby and more crucially consider how you're going to do this going forward. If your partner is off on maternity leave that may be coming to an end. Have you planned how to balance childcare and her returning to work, if she is? What are your plans with regards to work and your baby – can you work more flexibly or even work from home to share the load? Do you even want to consider it – or do you want to become a full-time father completely? (See Chapter 5 for more information about childcare options and Chapter 10 for discussion about flexible working and stay-at-home parenting.)

TEETHING

WHAT'S TEETHING ALL ABOUT?

Six months is around about the time that your child's gnashers will begin tearing their way through the gums and breaking open your baby's smile. That's right – six months. So pretty much at the moment you've got the feeding, sleeping and napping functions settled down then the teething troubles kick in.

Unless your baby has some strong Transylvanian genes in their pool then the first teeth to appear will be their incisors – the front two teeth. The pattern for growth will follow roughly this route:

6 months	Front incisors
7 months	Second (lateral) incisors
12 months	First molars (back teeth)
18 months	Canines (eye teeth)
24–36 months	Second molars
Three years old	Full set of 20 baby, or 'milk', teeth

These are ballpark figures – don't be too alarmed if your baby isn't displaying a gleaming set of ivory in their second birthday photos.

HOW DOES TEETHING AFFECT THE BABY?

The arrival of their first teeth can signal a series of reactions from your baby:

- Their gums can become inflamed.
- They'll produce saliva like they're a burst pipe.
- They'll chew at teething rings, toys, your fingers – whatever comes within their grasp.

Usually those first two teeth – the front incisors – don't give babies (and therefore parents) a huge amount of trouble. But the molars (busting through anytime from 12–19 months) come with a Parental Guidance warning. The signs that the molars are in town include hot and rosy red cheeks, tender gums, accompanied by an annoying sprinkling of disturbed sleep and grouchiness for the whole family.

Dad You Know?

The Whole Tooth

Your baby will eventually develop a full set of 20 milk teeth – 10 across the top and 10 at the bottom that'll serve them well enough, long enough for you to start saving for their tooth fairy windfall in a few years' time.

HOW CAN I HELP MY TEETHING TOT?

A dad can come to the rescue of his distressed dentally traumatised nipper in a number of ways – none of which will require the drills, fillings or the prerequisite 'you may feel a tiny prick'. Be prepared though, these may require you to dash out to a 24-hour chemist to purchase the following from the shelf marked 'God Sent':

- **Cool teething rings:** Pop this plastic ring in the fridge to magically unleash its temperature-reducing qualities. Take out. Apply to gob. Keeping it refrigerated means the cold gel inside the ring helps soothe the pain. (Feel free to apply this to your own head wounds next time you connect bonce with shelf.) The easy-to-grab handle prevents your baby's hands from getting cold – the lurid shades of these things ensure you don't lose them. (On the downside it establishes a link in your baby's mind between lurid liquids and happiness that will reprise in later life as they discover alcopops.)

- **Serve the drinks:** Again these will help with the inflammation and provide a less medicalised alternative to the Calpol or Calprofen that parents reach for to numb the pain. You can try rubbing your baby's gums gently too.
- **Make a mesh:** Mesh feeders are like a baby's dummy but with fruit and veg inside (you supply this bit) so that they can chew it without swallowing or more importantly without choking on bits.

SHOULD WE BRUSH OUR BABY'S TEETH?

At first it may help to soothe some of the pain caused by their emerging choppers by giving them a teething toy, but certainly once the teeth have come through – usually the bottom front ones first – you can brush them with a baby toothbrush (e.g. Aquafresh Milk Teeth toothbrush, Boots £2.10) and water initially. It's advisable not to use toothpaste until your child is old enough to know not to swallow it – at around two years of age.

Wisdom of Fathers

Teething Troubles

'I took a tip from my wife's mum on this one and would cool my son's gums by dipping my finger in a glass of water with a bit of ice in it while I help him on my lap. It meant he had nothing else in his mouth – just my finger and it seemed to work fine and cost nothing.' Patrick, father of Adam

'Emma, my partner, read up on all matters baby-related during pregnancy so when Joshua was teething she just started cutting up and chilling fruit – which I helped myself to as well. Chilled banana was easily the best way to deal with his teething and stop him crying when the gums were obviously sore for him.' Paul, father of Joshua

WEANING

WHAT IS WEANING?

Around this time – approximately six months old – your baby's compulsion to put anything in its mouth first will finally come in useful since they're now ready to start eating solids.

If you thought preparing baby formula was a chore, then prepare yourself for the delights of fruit mash, or baby-rice porridge.

To be fair it's a great opportunity for dads to take a hands-on role with feeding, especially if your other half has been breast-feeding all this time. You're going to be able to prepare meals and help your child develop a taste for the finer things in life like fresh vegetables, home-cooked meals and yes, even Brussels sprouts.

SHOULD I PURCHASE A HIGH CHAIR NOW?

There's a slightly surreal moment when you first plop your baby into a high chair to join you at the table for a meal. You can't help but laugh as for the first time since they were born they're now on a level with you – no longer being held in the recline position or sat in a low-level baby feeding chair, they're now eye to eye with you and ready to give you a whole new experience of table etiquette.

Despite all the modern advances in parenting paraphernalia, high chairs haven't changed a bit in centuries. Some museum and stately home antiquity high chairs share an uncanny resem-blance to your modern minimalist Scandinavian baby stool (check out the Eurobambino Natural Wooden high chair, for example).

Your baby should have the physical development to be able to sit in an upright position in a high chair at around six months. Ideally they'll be quite stable and controlled when seated – and will only bob about in the manner of Stevie Wonder occasionally.

If you can, it helps to get your little boy or girl used to sitting in the high chair before you start shifting their diet to solids. Key things to check when buying the high chair is:

- **Size:** Can you fit it in the car to take it home?
- **Construction:** Can you fit it together?
- **Safety:** Check that there's a safety restraint so that they can't slide out.
- **Hygiene:** Look for easy-to-clean trays and removable, washable seat covers.

HOW DO WE KNOW IT'S TIME FOR SOLIDS?

Your partner may give you some subtle clues that she wants to 'wean' your baby off liquids with statements like 'I can't go on breastfeeding anymore!' But other indicators from your very own babe will be:

- The aforementioned chomping of anything they can get their hands on.
- Being able to fully lift and support their head for long periods.
- Watching you gnawing on chicken wings and mimicking what you do.
- Draining your partner of milk in minutes and still demanding more.

The timing of weaning is not a precise science but if you're thinking of weaning before six months, talk to your health visitor or GP first as there are good reasons why the major health organisations recommend waiting this long. And be aware that you will have everyone from your mother to the postman telling you that you were chewing on baby rusks from three weeks old ...

Your baby won't go immediately from breast/bottle to a three-course *à la carte* menu – but it's a crucial stage in their development and over the next few months you'll find your own lives and schedules changing once more as their mealtimes begin to mirror your own. Don't expect the bottle feeds to stop overnight – your baby will still be taking liquids for many more months to come. They'll just be eating you out of house and home too.

WHAT'S BABY-LED WEANING (BLW)?

This pretty much does what it says in that your baby feeds itself – though it's not quite as simple as it sounds. Instead of the historic method of weaning your baby by introducing puréed food to its chops on a weaning spoon, your baby picks food up for itself – from a loose buffet provided by you – tastes them and then devours the ones it likes.

At this age they're grasping at things and will maybe gnaw on a cucumber stick without really eating it. But as your baby starts to get a taste for finger foods you may find that they take to baby-led weaning like a duck to water (though duck isn't an ideal option but you can try your baby with cooked meat and fish).

Dad You Know?

Bring Baby to the Table

Having a breakfast or evening meal at the table while your baby has a snack too, instead of sitting on the sofa with a TV dinner can help engender good habits. Research shows that children who sit down to eat dinner and talk with their family are far more confident communicators than those who don't. But the National Literacy Trust recently found that one in four children don't have a daily mealtime chat.

WHAT ARE THE BENEFITS OF BABY-LED WEANING?

Weaning is a great time for your family to start eating together no matter what way you do it. To see your baby sat at the table with you is another little landmark moment – don't be surprised if you find yourself taking photos when they first do it. Baby-led weaning has its own pros and cons:

- It's a useful way for your son or daughter to explore foods and get to grip – literally – with different textures.
- It's a whole lot easier than mushing food up into purées all the time.
- Parents who have tried BLW are generally quite positive about its benefits. They say their babies will eat anything and everything and that this helps to take the worry out of starting solids. But although there's plenty of anecdotal evidence about BLW, not much formal research has been done. One study did find that babies who are allowed to feed themselves from the beginning of weaning are more likely to join in with family mealtimes and eat a wide range of family foods early on.
- Aside from the taste, the texture of the food you're feeding him or her is a key contrast for them to get used to. Give them soft lumps of food to chew on around this time and they'll be lot more receptive to various types and flavours. But babies who aren't given lumpy food until a lot later – say around 10 months of age – are more likely to throw it back at you.

... And the cons?

Baby-led weaning is a much more messy experience for all involved than carefully, strategically shovelling one lot of mush into your baby. There can be quite a lot of waste too – it helps if you only give your baby a few pieces of food to mess about with at first.

Babies may find it hard to chew on some finger foods – and, no matter how quickly they're weaning, they're learning how to go from liquids to solids, so prepare for meals to take a lot longer than usual.

As with everything else babies develop at a different rate and often using puréed or well-mashed food is a handy bridge between liquid and solid foods. Usually by around six months babies can take feed off a spoon using their upper lip to drag the grub into their mouths – as opposed to the sucking motion they've been using since birth. But again be patient and prepare for some hiccups – both literally and metaphorically – as your baby progresses through the weaning stage. By around eight months, babies can usually chew and swallow foods with lumps.

WHAT KINDS OF FOODS SHOULD I GIVE MY BABY WHEN THEY'RE WEANING?

The easiest finger foods for young babies are those that are shaped like a chip (though it might be a good idea to go easy on actual chips right now). Instead, the dad of a weaning baby may like to pack the following when heading out into the world with junior:

- Sticks of cucumber (especially if teething as this will cool their gums too).
- Sticks of cheddar cheese.
- Carrot sticks (are you spotting the 'sticks' theme here?). These are best lightly cooked and then cooled at the beginning so that they are softer.
- Banana – broken into chunks.
- Rice cakes.
- Peach or nectarine chunks … oh go on then, or sticks.
- Steamed florets (poncy way of saying sticks) of broccoli.
- Pasta pieces (cooked then cooled).

WHAT FOODS SHOULD I NOT GIVE TO A WEANING BABY?

While good foods to choose for your baby in the early weaning stages are puréed fruits and vegetables and non-wheat cereals such as baby rice, there are also a few that the nutrition specialists suggest you don't put into the reach of hungry hands – or at least be very restrictive about giving them to your baby. Their immune system is still in the fragile stage so the following should be avoided before they're six months old:

- Eggs.
- Fish and shellfish.
- Soft and unpasteurised cheeses.

Other ingredients that really don't add to the whole weaning experience include salt – don't add it to food as it can put undue stress on their kidneys. Go easy on salty foods too – don't give them salty meats or snacks like crisps too often. Also sugary foods can increase the risk of tooth decay even before their pearly whites have broken through the gums, and parents are advised not to give babies honey for their first year.

WHAT'S THE BEST WAY TO ENSURE MY BABY EATS WELL?

Try to follow a few general weaning guidelines for the next, well, six months at least as they change their eating patterns and foods.

Think 'baby portions'

The nutrition experts and foretellers of such woes as the world obesity crisis have the right hump with portion sizes and they point a critical finger at (but fortunately not in) the portions of food we eat. Size is an issue and even at the baby end of the human growth cycle it's something to consider. A couple of teaspoons of baby rice or a chunk of fruit is usually plenty for a tiny baby who's just been used to fluids before this stage.

The idea is that you then gradually increase the amounts you give them as you pick up the signs that they're wanting more or they've had enough.

Check the temperature

Room temperature is ideal – so stir their food well and test it to check it's not too hot. You can actually get heat-sensitive baby spoons (£2.99 for three on Amazon) that change shade if the food is too hot.

Have a high chair

Feeding them on your lap may seem convenient – especially if there's something decent on TV – but it's not great for their digestion for starters. It's also a lot more likely that your carpet, sofa or shirt will end up as a 'menu' displaying the food your baby has eaten ... or spilled.

Clunk-click them in

Always strap your baby in securely, check that their fingers are clear of any attachments when you click the food tray in place and put a plastic floor mat beneath their high chair before they're in it.

Cover up

You can never have enough baby bibs – plus a good stock of baby spoons since they vanish just like adult spoons do.

Learn papa patience

Feeding your baby is all part of the bonding experience. It's a time when you can almost be guaranteed to have your baby's captive attention since they're fully focused on that spoonful of mixture that you're holding. But it's a big challenge for a baby to deal with solid foods and, as they get used to tasting and textures and trying not to choke themselves, you're going to have to let them take all the time they need. Even more so if you're baby-led weaning as it takes a long time to redecorate your walls with the food on offer.

Go with the flow

When they're older you can dictate when meals should start and end and when your child has had enough. At this age you're tied to the times they're hungry and to the routine that you've got them in to. When you know that time is approaching, get them seated and the food ready to go. When you take them out with you don't rely on others to be able to have their din-dins ready on time – instead pack snacks for them to nibble on until food arrives.

Go back with seconds

Weaning isn't solely about the transition from breast or bottle, or both, to eating finger foods and solid suppers. It's also about giving your child's diet variety and exposing them to tastes and flavours. The more varied and experimental these are the more chance there will be of them having wide, accommodating tastes when they get older too. Don't try them on a vindaloo just yet – but do dabble with foods that they reject first time, as they may come back to them later.

Add to the mix

Mixing foods with sauces is one way of getting babies to take in the nutrients in healthy food that they may be struggling with. When they're a little older and willing to chew on some sharper vegetables say, have a baby pasta sauce on hand too as a 'dip'.

Take note

Keep track of what you feed them. This isn't for some fancy dad's recipe book but simply so in the rare event that they have a reaction to their food – maybe a rash breaks out on their skin or they're suffering with a bout of diarrhoea – you may be able to trace the culprit.

Let them make a mess

When they want to grab the spoon and have a pop at feeding themselves (a bit of a way off yet) encourage them to do so. (Just have a spare spoon handy too.)

Stick with it

This really is a trial and error process and one that can test the temperament of the most saintly parents. As they grow they may react to some foods by smacking their hand down in the bowl or giving the 'choo-choo' spoon heaped with 'yum-yum' food a swift right hook. It may be that they don't like it. It could be that they're tired or they're just not hungry. Try the odd alternative food – desserts often go down better – this time around, or go back to something you know they usually enjoy. Put it down to experience; don't get annoyed or tell them off – it's all part of the process and hopefully the next meal won't be such a drama.

HOW DO I ENCOURAGE MY CHILD TO EAT HEALTHILY?

Dads influence their children in so many ways. Along with the more obvious mentoring, like teaching them tricks and skills, there's the subliminal influences too. Seeing you in and around the kitchen – cooking and eating healthily will rub off on your son or daughter too.

Not only is it crucial to keep your baby's diet healthy and varied as they grow but new parents need to take notice of what they're eating too. With a drain on your energy levels and demands on your mental and physical well-being it pays to make sure you're both eating a healthy, balanced diet.

If you're already a bit of a Gordon Ramsay in the kitchen – perhaps without his 'F' factor – then you'll be able to ensure there are some good home-made nutritional meals on the table as well as your partner. Sharing chores like this will ease the burden of parenthood, especially in the first months.

If you're not much of a cook then this is definitely the time to step up to the hot plate and became a modern dad with another skill in his armoury. A good starting point is the website www.mydaddycooks.com – devised by stay-at-home dad Nick Coffer, father of Archie, with a great selection of starter videos and recipes plus a book – created by a dad who started from scratch himself.

'We always wanted to help Archie have a good relationship with food, and when he turned six months and we began to wean him on to solids, we followed baby-led weaning – he ate at the table with us and ate what we were eating, when we were eating it.

'In the early days we had to ensure that his food was soft enough to chew but the principle remained the same. By no means at all does Archie eat everything, but he does engage with food and is curious about what we cook and eat.

'In reality, Archie has been "in" the kitchen since pretty well six months old, when he was hanging off my hip while I cooked.

'I set the blog up to simply document what and how we cook in our house. We try to eat fresh, healthy and interesting meals, using all manner of herbs, spices and ingredients, all cooked on a very modest budget.'

BONDING

AM I TURNING INTO MY DAD?

Research carried out in the US found that most parents say their expectations of being a parent changed dramatically after actually becoming parents. Being with a young baby can cause every idealistic parent to experience a short, sharp reality check.

Dads report that they change their idea about what being a parent entails soon after their baby comes along. In the study

Fatherhood Today: Men's Changing Role in the Family, many new fathers reported an increase in their contact with their own parents, especially their own dad. Of course some of this may have been down to the sudden rise in visits from happy grandparents-cum-babysitters. But many new dads did say that becoming a parent gives them a greater sense of maturity and that they felt they were viewed as being more 'grown up'.

When questioned about their own relationship with their fathers, a number of new dads responded by saying they were determined to make positive changes in their relationship with their own child. The upshot of the study was that the latter generation of fathers wanted to have stronger, closer relationships with their own children than they had experienced themselves.

WHY DO I FEEL DIFFERENT NOW I'M A FATHER?

Stress related to new parenthood, in fathers at least, appears to peak at around the time of the birth and first couple of months after the arrival of their newborn – often as the new dad tries to adapt to the physical, financial and emotional demands of it all.

In research into the effects of pregnancy and 18 months post-partum on fathers, researchers noted that men were most likely to display symptoms of postnatal depression around three to six months after their child was born.

As new fathers accept and shape their new role they're often observed to undergo some specific changes – fathers make fascinating subjects for sociological and psychological research too. New dads often:

- Develop more nurturing characteristics at work – that's right, you're softening up.
- Become more organised at home – now that there's someone making a greater mess than you.
- Become more adaptable and take a greater interest in the lives of those beyond the immediate circle of family and friends. Apparently the paternal instinct makes us fascinated with our colleagues' wild, child-free existences.

The *Fatherhood Today* study also revealed that in the first 18 months of their baby's life fathers reported a drop in the amount of quality time they spent with the mother of their child – while spending much more time with their infant. New parents were found to divide up home tasks more – with mothers doing more housework and dads cooking more than before.

WHAT WOULD I GET OUT OF TAKING A PARENTING COURSE?

With most positions of responsibility you have to go through some kind of training, apprenticeship or passing of exams. Whether it's for a rung up the career ladder or simply driving a car there are courses to be done and tests to take. Parenting however doesn't come with any statutory training required.

But it's a huge challenge, it's terribly hard work at times – incredibly rewarding at others – and each child–parent relationship is different. Some families are fortunate enough to have grandparents or other relatives on hand to pass on advice and give pointers on how things worked best for them. But for most couples becoming new parents, it's a case of learning on the job.

Fortunately there are some organisations run for first-time mums and dads – including ones that run father-only services and events – to help them learn how to become effective parents.

You may not feel that you need to be told how to be a dad, or that you don't want to ask for assistance because you don't want to be seen as struggling or unfit for duty. But parenting courses don't really work on the premise that you're not doing stuff right – they're more like trading places for 'best practice'.

Course tutors and other parents pass on tips for things that have worked for them in dealing with all types of situations – from teething and baby illnesses to dealing with finances and coping with relationship issues. Courses are often run with crèches or are open to bringing babies along too, so they'll get a chance to mix with others – they're often quite informal and, much like the dad's clubs that spring up (See Chapter 8), they provide a useful venue at which to exchange experiences and ideas.

To find parenting courses close to you, check out the following likely sources:

Children's centres

Local-authority funded centres not only offer support during pregnancy for mums and host breastfeeding classes but will also provide parental workshops for mums and dads together and separately, depending on the needs of the community, funding, take-up among parents and the availability of tutors. (Find contact details for your local centre from the government website, or phone 0870 000 2288.)

Positive parenting

Nationwide courses, leaflets and advice – including dad-focused programmes for early years – are arranged by www.careforthe-family.org.uk, which is part of a UK charity called Care for the Family.

NCT

You may have come across the NCT (National Childbirth Trust) in the antenatal stage of your parenting journey. They run a whole host of courses for new parents too including postnatal and CANparent classes along with Baby First Aid. Their website also has 'Dad's View' advice too – www.nct.org.uk

Parenting Matters and Parenting People

These websites offer online advice for dads and mums – www.parentingmatters.co.uk or www.parentingpeople.co.uk

HOW DOES BABY SIGN LANGUAGE WORK?

Research from the US National Institute of Child Health and Human Development shows that babies who learn to communicate through sign language can understand more words and develop a larger vocabulary in later life. But aside from being smarter and able to tell you more about what they want – watching your kid talk through sign language is also a great trick to keep you both entertained.

Children can pick up the basics of sign language from around seven months old, such as simple signs for 'milk' and 'sleep'. One father I spoke to, Matt Sanders, taught his baby to use sign language and by 18 months old she could use 42 different signs. Some experts are wary that too much focusing on sign language can take priority over speech development. Other anecdotal endorsements from parents suggest that babies who learn to sign are less prone to tantrums and learn to communicate through speech a lot sooner than siblings who don't learn to sign.

Some national organisations like www.singandsign.com provide classes around the UK for parents and babies to attend. Alternately you can begin teaching your nipper to learn at home using simple steps like the way you teach your baby to wave 'goodbye'.

- Baby recognises Daddy waving goodbye.
- Baby starts to imitate you when you wave.
- Baby starts to wave spontaneously as you get ready to leave – this is when a baby is instigating its own communication by signing.
- Baby learns to say the words 'bye-bye' while waving.

The common signs are pretty self-explanatory. Hold an open palm against your head – imitating a pillow – for 'sleep'. Tip your thumb to your mouth for 'drink' or 'milk' – whereas others like rubbing your hand on your belly for 'bath' (mimicking drying yourself with a towel) are a lot more user-friendly for a nine month old than trying to replicate your own specific bath-room tap arrangement.

Wisdom of Fathers

Signs of a Connection

'I read about teaching babies to communicate via sign language in a newspaper article and tried some of the signs out with my daughter Julia when she was nine months. The signs were very basic but I was attracted to the idea of being able to "converse" with Julia and help her communicate her needs to us beyond crying. She learnt quickly and I remember the day I was upstairs and she was at the bottom of the stairs. She pulled herself up on the stair gate and rubbed her belly with one hand (the sign for "bathtime") then rubbed her hand against her ear (sign for bed) – I couldn't believe it, she wasn't even a year old and was telling me she wanted to have a bath then go to bed!' Richard, father of Julia and Miles

---

WHAT ELSE CAN I DO TO BOND WITH MY CHILD?

Be the talking book

Long before your baby is old enough to tune out to an audio book you will be the voice they hear and associate with magical stories, fantasies and wonderful worlds. Start reading to them when they're born – or before if you can get over the weirdness of chatting to your partner's bump.

Be a carrier

Get used to taking your baby out with you whenever you're at home. It can give your partner a break and help you and them get to know each other a lot more. Taking a buggy or wearing them in a carrier will bring you both – literally – closer together. Skin-to-skin contact is great for inducing a biological bond between a baby and papa – great if done at home on the sofa on a lazy Sunday afternoon but not such a good move in the coffee shop on a Saturday morning.

Be the record keeper

Take photos, write blogs, collect the drawings they do and things they make to reinforce that attachment between you. Parents treasure these keepsakes and children will realise the true value of them in later life too. Plus they're fun to wheel out when the child is an adult to embarrass them in front of their new girl- or boyfriend.

7

HEALTH, SAFETY AND FITNESS

Child's Life: Weeks 25–28

WHAT'S HAPPENING WITH OUR BABY AT THIS STAGE?

Though they will be making sounds that are more like little babbling noises, he or she is having a damn good go at speaking the way you do. They're still a way from speaking their first 'words' as such – that usually occurs from around 11 months onwards – but they're babbling away, making vowel sounds and the odd consonants too in their own little version of *Countdown*. Other foibles of the seven-month-old baby may include:

- Reaching for things and lunging forwards.
- Making their first crawling movements.
- Standing up while holding chairs, table legs – or your leg for that matter.
- Sitting up without support.

They could be communicating with waves or by banging objects together in each hand, though that's more for their own enjoyment than any other reason.

SHOULD WE LET OUR BABY HAVE A DUMMY?

There's a big debate on the plusses and pitfalls of giving your baby a dummy (also called soothers or, in the USA, a pacifier) to suck on.

On the upside, it can do what it says on the tin – soothing or pacifying your baby when they're particularly grouchy. On the downside some experts warn that excessive dummy sucking – for six hours a day or more – can knacker a baby's developing teeth. It may also prevent your baby from 'babbling' – part of its speech development. And it acts as a decoy, meaning that parents may miss the underlying reason for their baby's crying.

If you're going to use one it's a good idea to be selective as to when and how you use it. Definitely don't dip it into sweet stuff to make your kid 'take' it, and try to get your baby off using it once it's weaned on to solid foods or ideally by the time it's one year old. To wean them off it, try giving them a substitute comforting device like a blanket or a cuddly toy.

SHOULD WE SWITCH TO A PUSHCHAIR?

As your baby gets more and more comfortable with sitting upright you may find it useful to switch from the pram or buggy you've used to a forward-facing pushchair. It's a good idea to check the manufacturer's guidelines for the correct minimum age or weight of child before plonking them in one – babies under six months should have a pushchair that gives their head plenty of support and has a five-point harness too. (This is ultra-secure – think parachute harness.) If they're able to sit upright unsupported then a pushchair shouldn't be a problem for them now.

I'M KNACKERED, WHY IS THIS BABY WEARING ME OUT?

More than ever, you're in demand. As a new dad you're a mentor, supporter, breadwinner (possibly the only one), carer, play-friend, tutor, cook, cleaner, bather and counsellor for your partner and baby. Many of these will be roles you're taking on for the first time. All this extra-curricular activity requires a man who's on top of his game. New dads will often cite the arrival of their first child as having a positive effect on their own health.

Quit the cigarettes

If you haven't already, now's definitely the time to quit. Look at it from your baby's point of view. US research from 2012 shows that if 'your father smoked while you were a baby your genes are most likely damaged and your odds for cancers and other diseases could be increased.' Check out your nearest quit-smoking advice centre where puffing papas can access smoking cessation products and advice – www.nhs.uk/livewell/smoking

Beware the back

Along with lifting your baby and the vast array of accessories that comes with them, new dads need to take care when going on the road. 'Car seat fitting can be a major cause of back problems for new parents,' explains Dr Jenny Sutcliffe, physiotherapist and author of *The Back Bible* (Bloomsbury). Both new mums and dads report to their GPs with new-baby-related back issues – often due to poor lifting and carrying techniques. 'When putting your baby in the car or just putting the buggy in the boot try not to bend over,' says Dr Sutcliffe. 'The most common cause of injury is bending and twisting so instead get into the car with your baby in its seat and fit it without having to bend or twist.'

Keep on running

A double whammy for dads to help build the bond and stay or get into shape comes with the relatively new craze of running with your baby. These days some baby buggies have been specially designed for just this purpose – see the BOB Ironman

Jogging Stroller (bobgear.com) if you don't believe me. It's not recommended that you run with your little one until they are at least six months of age. And when you do, it pays to take into account some simple 'running with baby' rules (see page 149).

=== Dad You Know? ===

The Long, Long Road

Eighty-seven per cent of parents push their buggies between 3 and 10 miles per week. (Maclaren)

FIT AND HEALTHY

HOW DO I STAY FIT AS A FATHER?

Becoming a dad is the biggest incentive for overweight men to shed the pounds – that's what a survey of 1,000 men carried out by Weight Watchers revealed in 2013. It also suggested that men are more likely to go on a diet when they have a new baby than if their doctor told them to lose weight or if they were trying to impress the opposite sex.

More than a third (37 per cent) wanted to get fitter so they could enjoy a kick around with their children, while 31 per cent of men asked said they'd lose weight to set a good example, and 11 per cent wanted to compete with other dads at the school gates.

All well and good of course – until Weight Watchers cut to the chase (or just highlighted why they're commissioning this kind of thing). It turns out that almost half of UK dads – 45 per cent – are overweight and at risk of health issues such as heart disease and diabetes.

But staying in shape isn't easy if you've a hectic life of work and a family to raise – devoting time to achieve fitness goals can become tricky. And as a dad there's a few 'habits' you find yourself getting into; for example new dads celebrating Father's Day are much more likely to opt for sedentary pastimes – like a meal out, at a pub, followed by a night on the sofa watching a film – instead of healthy outdoor activities like a family bike ride.

HOW CAN I AVOID 'FAT FATHER' SYNDROME?

As a former marine-turned-fitness trainer and performance director with Balance Physiotherapy, Jonathan Lewis has taken a personal involvement in getting fathers fitter. 'As a dad myself I know how easy it can be to fall foul of weight gain or getting out of condition when the kids come along,' says Lewis. 'I've worked with a lot of athletes looking to maintain a family and fitness balance and have found that it really isn't down to just making a couple of trips to the gym every week. You need to apply the rules 24/7. This may sound tough on top of everything else you're doing as a new dad, but in reality it's just about spreading out the load and incorporating good diet and movement into your everyday life.'

Watch out for waist gain

'Instead of the same old advice on monitoring portion sizes and eating five-a-day – rather than taking a defensive approach of avoiding weight gain, go a step further,' says Lewis. 'Aggressively pursue a healthier, more sustainable lifestyle. This will benefit the whole family. Start it now and your children will learn habits of eating and hydrating they will not learn at school.'

'If you don't do it already, take control of the weekly shopping – buy real food, use the Internet for raw foods and superfoods, shop for organic and locally produced fruit, vegetables, eggs, meat and milk. Eating healthily is easier than ever.'

To pursue a fitter father lifestyle Lewis recommends some bedtime reading material too: '*The Health Delusion* by Aidan Goggins and Glen Matten is a great start, or *Fitter Food* by Keris Marsden and Matt Whitmore – they have simple, practical and easily implemented health-changing ideas.'

'Instead of mine-sweeping and consuming the leftover scraps that your children reject scoop it straight into the bin,' suggests Lewis. 'This becomes less important if you are feeding your children good quality food rather than industrialised baby products – home-produced hand-blended vegetables and quality chicken for example that are blitzed and frozen in ice-cube trays may be on the bland side, but they will be healthy and nutritious and in small portions.'

--- *Dad You Know?* ---

Lost Days

Ninety per cent of British parents claim they lose up to 28 hours of sleep every week – that's 60 days per year! (Pampers)

What kind of exercise should I be doing then?

Perhaps the best way to stay in shape in the early months of parenthood is to find some activities that dovetail nicely into your life.

- There are the usual tips like take the stairs instead of the lift. This is never easy when you're out with a baby in a buggy so maybe save that one for work days only.
- If walking out helps settle your baby then make it part of their routine with you – or even just strap them into a baby carrier and take yourself out for a 30-minute walk in the evening or during the day at weekends.
- Take turns in having a night off the sofa. You and your partner can take turns in pursuing those pastimes you both enjoyed before baby came along – or else take the opportunity to meet up with new-found parent friends for some socialising without having Baby in tow.
- Where possible walk or cycle reasonable distances rather than taking the car. You don't really need to be told that I know. However as a dad who likes to cycle you may be

tempted to combine a bit of the Bradley Wiggins life with a spot of babysitting. Although you can get child seats for the back of bikes, it's a bit too early at this stage to be plonking your child into one. Infants vary a lot as to the age at which they are able to sit up unaided – which is when they are ready to ride in a bicycle child seat. (Though they may be doing this a little already they don't usually do it with much control until they're about nine months old.)

- Home gym equipment like the rowing machine or the exercise bike or even a jump rope may come in handy around this time. Check out sites like eBay for such gear being sold by other well-intentioned but defeated dads.
- You could invest in a bicycle trailer. With similar age/ weight/development restrictions as the baby seat it's possibly not something for right now, but further down the line it could be useful. Some dads find them really helpful for taking kids out with them when running errands or going to the park. Others find the thought of poodling along a dual carriageway with your offspring hooked to the back of your bike as lorries and buses thunder past marginally insane. It's your call, Dad.

'While you are at it change your approach to fitness and movement,' suggests Lewis. Health, strength, vitality and wellness are not achieved through isolated events at the gym, in your garage, or during exertions on the football or rugby pitch once every weekend. 'It is, like fatherhood itself, a full-time adventure. Exploration is the key – keep active and move every day, with full and rhythmical movements utilising as much as your body as possible. "Open" and "close" the main areas of the body – shoulders, trunk (spine and ribcage) and hips.'

HOW DO I GO RUNNING WITH A BABY?

Father, runner and sports writer Rob Spedding passes on his advice for dads looking to take their nipper for a dash.

Running with the pushchair is much harder than running alone because of the added resistance. 'Universities are very good at studying the obvious – like the Texas A&M University – "discovered" that running with additional load of a baby in a buggy provided a more intense workout,' says Spedding. 'Make that workout even more intense by carrying some essential kit too: a screwdriver, Allen key, pump and puncture repair kit – plus nappies, wipes and food for your baby.'

Do some warm-ups

Get used to losing your natural arm swing when you run – and keep the safety strap of your pushchair on one of your wrists. 'If your baby's head still wobbles like Paula Radcliffe then they're not ready to run yet,' says Spedding. Only when they have head control, can sit up and also handle the bouncing of the pushchair should you think about it.

Get a pushchair that's intended for jogging

Go for one with a five-point harness, bike-style handbrakes, air-filled wheels that are at least 40.5 cm (16 in) diameter and a cover to protect your baby from the sun and stop insects hitting them in the face.

Kiddicare.com also features buggies like the Mountain Buggy MB2 for around £490, or you can find a wider selection of off-roaders at stockists like www.babyjogger.co.uk

Wisdom of Fathers

Walking With Babies

'We made a significant mistake early on – we thought we had it made because Elias slept so much in the day when we were out walking in the Peaks – he'd sleep for hours on end in the carrier. Looking back, I think this meant he reversed day and night. He slept for long periods in the day but only briefly at night. We should have put a routine in place much earlier and woken him up if necessary during the day. It took us three months to figure out what was going on.' Mike Jones, father of Elias

SAFETY AND FIRST AID

HOW DO I BABY-PROOF MY HOME?

Now that your wee one is getting close to touring the floor on all fours – if he or she isn't already – then it may be time for you to join them down there and take a view of the world from a baby's eye level. What you're looking for is anything dangerous to a crawling, staggering, inquisitive baby – so sharp edges, easy-to-swallow hazards and electrical sockets.

Yep, it's time to baby-proof your home.

There are two ways to do this. One is to ramp up the child protection devices and safeguarding gadgets you use as your child gets older and more adroit at terrifying you as they learn through experience. Or you could just blitz the house now and cover as many death-traps as you can in one fell swoop.

With this in mind here's the kinds of things the Royal Society for the Prevention of Accidents advise new parents to look out for in order that they don't become a RoSPA statistic:

Electrical sockets

There is some debate as to the true hazard of the modern generation of sockets and the likelihood of a child really getting a shock from them. However some parents prefer the peace of mind that comes with covering up the power points. (six covers, £1.99 at www.babysecurity.co.uk)

Electrical cabling

In particular you need to look out for those wires and cables that overhang worktops, or ones that are not coiled or extendable. Cordless gadgets can be a safer option at this time. Look out for any leads under tables or sofas, etc. that a teething child could chomp on too.

Cabinet doors

Safety latches (12-pack at www.mothercare.com, £6.99) on bathroom, kitchen and living room cabinets and drawers keep inquisitive fingers from getting trapped and potentially poisonous or breakable products away from the wrong hands. Great for when friends visit and can't fathom out how to open the drinks cabinet too.

Lock down the loo

An intriguing one this, and one which most dads will just laugh at and think 'no way'. That is until they're the ones having to fish a dummy, favourite toy or their smart phone out of the U-bend. So install toilet locks to keep toilet lids closed. In all seriousness, toddling children are more top-heavy than adults – as most *You've Been Framed!* clips featuring babies will confirm. A walking wee one can topple head first into toilets.

Get into the habit

Although your little babe's barely seven months old, those months will have passed quickly no doubt. The next ones will too and before you know it they're 'into everything'. Get used to unplugging electrical stuff and certainly taking extra care when cooking. Use the stove's back burners and turn pan handles toward the back of the stove to keep hot pots out of the reach of children.

Cover up

Put corner and edge bumpers (Mothercare eight-pack, £5.99) on furniture and other items like a fireplace hearth to protect against injury.

Cut the cord

Watch out for window blinds with looped cords – they can be strangulation hazards for children. Also check out any free-falling lids on toy chests or storage boxes.

Get a gate

Safety gates at the top and bottom of stairs are something to look out for now even before your baby's anywhere near walking – partly because they're such a bugger to fit and it's good to get some practice in. But also because you can get very good condition pre-loved ones at events like nearly new baby-gear sales, online and at car boot fairs. Be sure to measure the doorway width of any room you're looking to seal off – gates with expanding pressure bars should not be used for blocking the top of stairs.

Dad You Know?

Kids and Kitchens

While you're getting into the habit of making your home a safe haven for toddlers it's worth investigating things like oven locks in the kitchen – or ideally putting a gate separating that room from the rest when they're older. Take care not to put pet food, cat litter trays or mouse traps in places where your child will be able to get at them. Household plants and bulbs – from irises to daffodil bulbs are toxic to humans and should be kept out of the reach of little ones. Fireplaces should be screened off with a guard, and where possible avoid leaving anything in waste baskets or bins that could be harmful to your baby.

WHAT FIRST-AID STUFF DO WE NEED NOW WE'VE GOT A BABY?

Since we're covering the many ways to try to prevent a moving child from becoming an accident statistic, let's also look at what you need to have at home to cover some eventualities too. We'll call it 'father's first-aid kit', though it's basically there for anyone to use – and the idea is that it's for dealing with the minor mishaps. With babies especially it's always safest to err on the side of caution and get any worrying aliments, falls or illnesses to your doctor ASAP. In the meantime a few essentials to stock up on are:

1 Plasters

There are even baby-friendly ones of these. Instead of the rough flesh-colour Elastoplast ones you and I probably had stuck to us after a collision with the coffee table as a toddler, babies can now get TV character plasters – the Peppa Pig Plasters (18 pack at www.boots.com, £2.99) are especially good at treating a wound and making the pain go away a little quicker.

2 Bruise smoother

These are ideal for bumps and knocks your baby may incur – and any whacks you receive yourself for that matter. This is a gel inside a plastic case often shaped like a kid's cartoon character. (Peppa Pig has cornered this market too, though the Mr Men are also muscling in on the action – the Mr Bump one is especially apt.) You leave it to chill in the fridge and then apply to a bump to reduce the swelling and pain as and when you need to. (Which seems to be every hour once they start toddling.)

3 Thermometer

What a baby can't tell you themselves about how they're feeling, a quick check of their temperature can usually communicate easily enough. Baby thermometers work on reading the temperature via the baby's ear. Braun produce a 'ThermoScan ExacTemp' ear thermometer that can provide a reading without even waking your baby up.

4 Skin cream

Itchy spots, mild rashes, heat rashes, nappy irritation, carpet burns – the list goes on. As the mass of sun-protection goods for babies will confirm, their skin is more sensitive than the average car alarm and can break out in a reaction at any time to the slightest trigger. Keep a soothing cream in the first-aid kit – calamine lotion is good – but check its label to avoid aggravating any skin condition like eczema.

5 Nappy rash cream

Nappy rash is one of the most common 'complaints' for your baby. It's not a sign of poor hygiene or bad parenting, simply a side effect of being a baby and doing a lot of wee, randomly, through the day. Nappy rash creams like Sudocrem are antiseptic so they help prevent things getting worse and protect the skin from the next stream of baby by-product.

6 Calpol

Before fatherhood it's unlikely you'll have even heard of this product. Within a few months of parenthood you will know this to be a miracle cure elixir that you never leave home without. It's basically nice-tasting paracetamol in a format that a baby can tolerate (from about the age of two months upward). Ideal for helping to reduce fever and relieve pain, it's pretty much the first thing you should have on your first-aid kit list. (Why then have I put it down here at number 6?)

7 Calgel teething gel

This one's specially formulated to treat sore gums – the nauseating side effect of your baby having their first teeth coming through. It's a gel to rub on those inflamed areas of the mouth in the desperate hope that their gums will get some cooling, your little one will get some relief and you'll get some bloody sleep at last. Always read the label.

8 Decongestant

Adult males have evolved a series of gross manoeuvres to relieve their sinuses of snot, bogeys and all manner of congestants. Sadly wee babies have so much to learn, so for the moment they need a little help. Baby decongestants are used to help them breathe easier when they get the sniffles. The idea is that you apply this stuff to a muslin square (the weird cloth thing that only babies seem to have) and leave it near them when they're sleeping to help clear their airways. The cloth shouldn't be left within their reach though.

Dad You Know?

First-Year Aid

According to a survey from www.findababysitter.com, 7 out of 10 parents in the UK admit to not knowing how to help their child in a medical emergency situation.

SHOULD I DO A FATHER'S FIRST-AID COURSE?

Once your baby starts making themselves mobile by crawling, cruising and walking so a whole new world is opened up to them. Unfortunately that world is also full of potential dangers and the risk of your kid coming a cropper around the house multiplies.

—————————— *Wisdom of Fathers* ——————————

First-Aid Courses

'I'd done some first-aid training before but it wasn't specific to children and I found that it's really useful to get some training that focused on the problems babies and toddlers may have because some of the techniques are a bit different. I chose to do it after our baby had a breath-holding attack – stopping himself breathing until he turned blue and passed out. Fortunately the paramedic came quickly – though we had to wait an age for the follow-up ambulance to arrive. It's not uncommon for babies to do this but when it happens to your child for the first time you feel powerless to deal with it. I booked myself on to a first-aid course with the Red Cross soon after that. It was aimed at parents though there were only a couple of dads – one of them was an English guy who'd flown in from Russia to learn baby first aid because the emergency facilities over there are so bad! I've since recommended the course to other dads. You learn about dealing with issues like breath-holding along with treating accidents like choking and poisoning. It gives you the confidence and peace of mind you need to know that you'll be able to treat your child if there is a problem in the future. It's probably the best £45 I've spent.' Johnny, father of Tommy at 14 months

According to RoSPA more than one million children under the age of 15 experience accidents in and around the home every year – with those most at risk from a home accident in the 0–4 years age group.

New dads can sign up to first-aid courses specifically tailored to deal with common injuries sustained by babies and children. These courses are run by a number of organisations. To find your nearest one check out the following:

- The British Red Cross offer courses direct to parents www.redcrossfirstaidtraining.co.uk
- The NCT run a baby first-aid course delivered by quali-fied Red Cross trainers, (www.nct.org.uk).

WHAT SHOULD I DO IF OUR BABY HAS A FEVER?

It's not at all uncommon for your child to experience a rise in temperature as their immune system continues to develop – especially as they come into contact with more and more children.

If they're under three months old it's advisable to contact your baby's doctor straight away. With older children it's a case of observing how they're reacting to their temperature. Some of them will merrily play along as before, despite having a hot flush. Use a few cooling ploys to make them comfortable.

- **Cool room:** Keep their bedroom and their cot at a comfy temperature – and don't wrap them up too snugly. A vest and nappy may suffice for now.
- **Cool drinks:** Give them plenty of cool fluids – boiled water that has been cooled down or well-diluted squash.
- **Cool medicine:** If you're used to giving your baby a temperature-reducing medicine (like Calpol Infant Suspension) this may help. Follow the instructions but if there's no significant change in 24 hours take your baby to their GP.

HOW SHOULD I DEAL WITH BABY EMERGENCIES?

A recent survey found that 70 per cent of parents have taken their baby or child to an A&E unit at some point, while 83 per cent believe that they would feel more confident in giving first-aid treatment if they had instant access to guidance.

Sometimes the quickest way to get medical help for your

baby is to take them directly to your local A&E – don't be too alarmed if you get a bit familiar with this place in the early years of fatherhood.

If you can learn the basics of first aid though, it'll possibly save you trips to casualty and at least give you the peace of mind of knowing that should anything serious befall your little one you'll be able to step in and provide practical help if your baby needs it.

Some of the more common problems to affect children at this age include:

Choking

'If your baby is unconscious, first check if they are breathing. If they are breathing call an ambulance,' explains Jane Keogh, a first-aid specialist with the British Red Cross.

Hold the baby in your arms with their head tilted downwards and supported. Effective back blows cure the majority of choking incidents – other procedures to follow include:

- Check inside their mouth and remove any visible obstructions. Do not sweep the mouth with your finger to search for an obstruction.
- Lay them face down with their head lower that their bottom along your forearm. Support their head and shoulders with your hand. Give up to five back blows between their shoulder blades with the heel of your hand.
- Turn them face up along your other arm. Check their mouth again. If there is an obvious obstruction then remove it with your forefinger and thumb.
- Give up to five chest thrusts. Place two fingers on the lower half of the baby's breastbone and push inwards and upwards towards their head. Then check the mouth again.

If the blockage has not cleared repeat two further cycles of back blows and chest thrusts. If the baby is still choking call 999.

Burns and scalds

Put the affected area under cold running water for at least 10 minutes – then cover with cling film or a clean pillow case. For any burn or scald to a baby seek medical advice.

Meningitis

Although it's a rare illness, meningitis causes inflammation of the brain lining which can be fatal. Its symptoms are flu-like so it can easily be mistaken for something much more innocent. Look out for:

- A high temperature.
- A more high-pitched cry than usual.
- Repeated vomiting.
- A swelling or tightness of the fontanelle – the soft spot on the top of the baby's head.
- Drowsiness or floppiness.
- A blotchy red/purple rash which does not fade when you try the 'glass test' – where you press a glass against it.

If you suspect your baby does have meningitis, call 999 or take your baby to your nearest A&E department.

Thinking of your child in an emergency situation is not a nice thought for any parent. But taking a first-aid course and regularly topping up your first-aid skills means you'll be calm and confident if you are ever faced with an emergency.

There's also a free British Red Cross Baby and Child First Aid app – which features advice and skills that only take a few minutes to learn but could save a life www.redcross.org.uk/babyandchildapp

COMMUNICATION

HOW DO I CHAT TO A SEVEN MONTH OLD?

Even at this stage your baby will be beginning to understand the meaning of language and the idea of using their voice to communicate – even if they don't specifically get what you're saying. The best example of this is that your baby will start responding to their name – at least turning their head toward you when you say it and so distinguishing it from other words.

They could even have a bit of a grasp on the 'no' command as well. They may not always follow the instruction but it's likely that they're picking up from the sharp directness of the tone you attach to it that 'no' isn't an encouragement to them to continue with whatever it is they're doing or chewing.

On the nonverbal-communication front they're making great strides around this time too. Investigate learning baby sign language at this time too (see Chapter 6). They're most likely be gurning, grinning, frowning and blowing raspberries at you fairly regularly now too. They'll do this more and more as their memory is developing, and they'll have recall of what your face looks like when you're happy and when you're not.

They also develop an understanding of the permanence of objects around this age too – in other words they realise that just because they can't see something doesn't mean it's not out of their mind. With this can come what's called separation anxiety – they may be upset when Mum especially leaves the room. Stranger anxiety can also kick in around this time too.

As a new dad you may find that your partner tries to schedule any trips out around the time your baby is napping – you could be left holding the sleeping baby, just to ease some of their anxiety. Otherwise you should also get used to creating distractions and playing with toys and the like to keep your baby occupied and comfortable while your partner leaves the room, pops out for a while or just nips to the toilet.

These landmark developments in your baby's personality are wonderful to witness but can also be a strain on you both as parents, understandably upset at seeing your little one unhappy too. Reassure each other that is all part of the parenting process, that there's no serious long-term damage occurring and that you're not bad parents because your baby is just doing what babies are meant to do.

8 JOIN THE CLUB

Child's Life: Weeks 29–32

WHAT'S HAPPENING WITH OUR BABY AT THIS STAGE?

They're coming up to eight months! Where did that go? It will quite possibly have flown by as your little girl or boy will have been a rollercoaster ride of growth spurts, liquids and solids, as well as near-constant movement and protection against all that's too cold, too hot, too loud and too bright. As ever with a caveat of 'your child at this stage could be ...' here's some of the things they *could* be doing around about now:

- They may well be crawling around a lot and working their way up off all fours and then standing while holding on to something, or someone.
- They may try 'cruising' around furniture by holding on and shuffling.
- For your sake I hope they're sleeping – as they should be – around 10–12 hours a day.
- They're gripping tighter and clutching things with a tight squeeze.
- You may notice them 'gathering' toys – a habit many get into as they become toddlers.

- Their reactions will be quickening and they may make some messy attempts at feeding themselves with a bottle or cup.
- Babbling could be featuring more and more as they master their communication skills.
- Pointing at things they want might happen too.

Don't be alarmed if your baby isn't tearing around the floor on all fours just yet though. Each baby follows their own development path and, though it's tempting to get a bit competitive about how well your child is doing, there's no definitive rule as to what your baby should be doing and when. Do carry on reading aloud to them and definitely play music to them – they have a great ear for rhythm and it's been shown to help in their learning too.

HOW DO I RUB MY BABY UP THE RIGHT WAY?

Baby massage has become a staple among the features of the posh parenting magazines. Don't be put off by the idea that it's some weird alternative wizardry though. It's a simple skill to learn, though there's more to it than meets the eye. And bear in mind that even at this age your baby can be quite a discerning customer – some babies just don't dig massage at all. But for many babies and their parents it can be a wonderful, stress-reducing and bonding experience.

When should I do baby massage?

'For the first six weeks of life we need to be held, rubbed, rocked and spoken to while we 'gather our senses' in a new and an unfamiliar environment,' reveals Peter Walker, practitioner and tutor of the chillaxing art of baby rubbing (www.babymassageteachertraining.com).

'For those first six weeks baby massage should be done whenever, wherever, with the baby clothed, and is a good introduction to massage,' says Walker.

Dad You Know?

Massaging – The Statistics

A huge study published in laugh-on-every-page bedside read *The Journal of Perinatal Education* found that infant massage has proved to be a very useful way for dads to get up to speed with their 'caregiving sensitivity' – which doesn't sound like the most alpha male of additions to the modern dad's skill set but has some very positive knock-on effects.

Researchers found that through taking part in baby massage sessions, a small group of new dads were helped by increasing their feelings of competence, role acceptance, spousal support, attachment and health and by decreasing feelings of isolation and depression.

All that from simply rubbing your baby's limbs with some lotion and muttering some kind words in the process. Although not all fathers saw the direct benefit of infant massage – they did all say they enjoyed participating in an activity that gave them special time with their kids and appreciated the opportunity to meet other fathers.

The study helped to highlight the fact that fathers are more than capable of being engaged parents, and father–infant massage may represent a valuable tool to assist fathers in that regard.

Secondly, infant massage was seen to be an effective way to engage dads and improve their parenting experiences – even in the face of potential increases in general life stresses such as financial burden, fatigue and relationship strain. Finally, infant massage classes appear to offer fathers the positive experience of meeting other men in the same boat and enjoying the opportunity to share their fathering experiences.

'A gentle massage using stroking techniques and a fruit or vegetable oil can be introduced following bathtime,' suggests Walker. 'Oils like sunflower oil, grapeseed or a light olive oil can be used for dry skin – always do a skin test first to ensure the baby is not allergic to the oil you've chosen, and avoid mineral-based commercial baby oils.'

Although there's something of a knack to it, the fundamental moves involve gently rubbing each limb – getting you both used to the hormone-fizzing positive side effects of touch.

'To start, use the oil like you would soap, just to get the feel of your baby and allow your baby to get the feel of you,' says Walker. 'A more formal routine like Developmental Baby Massage can be introduced later, about 8–10 weeks.' Some basic rules to remember when doing a baby massage are:

- Use a double bath towel on a safe surface.
- Always stop immediately if your baby cries.
- It could be they are feeling too vulnerable, unwell, not in the mood, cold, hungry – it does not mean that they do not like being touched. Give them what they want and then try again.

'Massage allows dads and babies to literally "get in touch" with each other,' says Walker. 'The way we hold and touch our babies and children tells them all that they need to know about how loved and wanted they are. It also allows men to develop the softer, more compassionate side of our nature.'

If you do a course in it you learn specific massage strokes for their legs, feet, arms, face, stomach and back. You'll find out the oils to use, ways to adapt the massage as they grow and a few specific routines to help treat issues like colic.

WHAT WOULD I GET OUT OF GOING ALONG TO A DAD'S CLUB?

The last of the three findings from the infant massage study on page 164 also reveal how new dads can master the role a lot quicker if they're able to share best practice, ideas and in some cases just cluelessness with other dads. And why not? Many new mums will tell you that they pick up much of what they're applying from other new mums they've met through postnatal groups, coffee mornings, baby massage or swim sessions.

Because all babies are different it really is a trial and error process for new parents. While there are plenty of books out there – possibly too many some may argue – more and more of us take notice of 'reviews' from peers. We'll do it for holiday resorts via websites like TripAdvisor. We'll take note of what other people say when recommending books or restaurants or pretty much anything you want to buy online these days, so why not parenting advice too?

For thousands of years new mums have taken the lead on this – trying out a method to deal with a baby-related matter that another mum has had success with. Nowadays there are facilities for new dads to do the same and get other benefits too: Dad's Clubs. 'Like a bunch of blokes in a pub – but without the booze and with your kids.' That's how one father summed up his use of a group specially designed for fathers to share some quality time with their kids – but often with a sideline in sound advice for the new dad too.

Jay Blades runs the Men Behaving Dadly scheme in Brentford, West London. At Men Behaving Dadly, new fathers are encouraged to bring their children along to a Saturday or Sunday morning session of activities and baby banter. 'The youngest child we've had come in with their dad was around three weeks old,' says Blades. Usually though, it's children from eight months and older that come through the door with their at-first-wary dads. 'We keep it very informal, initially providing them with a setting to do crafts, play games and generally spend some time together.'

Blades' scheme includes dads working shifts and those separated from their child's mother.

'We'll do "day out" activities to the local play centre, to the park and we have an allotment session where they use grow bags to produce their own plants and food,' says Blades. 'The dads not only get to play with their children but they'll swap advice with other fathers too. We can also provide some advice and guidance on issues regarding parenting too – or else point them in the right direction. The dads get a great deal out of the sessions and the feedback we get is good.'

As well as helping fathers to bond with their children the sessions provide a relaxed atmosphere for children to play with other kids and for dads to socialise with each other. One of the fathers who attended Blades' group explained: 'I was finding it really difficult to deal with my son's behaviour. He was very active, challenging and exhausting. I was at my wits' end, and it was affecting my other children and my wife. Attending MBD has been wonderful. I have felt comfortable talking to the other dads about the problems we have been dealing with, and they have been a great support to us all. Coming to the sessions has taught me to play differently with my children and I don't get frustrated anymore.'

How do I find a Dad's Club nearby?

Dads 'n' Little 'Uns, Who Let The Dads Out?, Men Behaving Dadly – don't fear, somewhere out there there's a group for you, and the only bad thing about it will be the contrived pun it has as its name.

Sadly there's no central database for the dad groups in the UK – though many use local authority play centres and children's centres for their meetings. Try your local civic centre or children's services department first. Ask at any nearby infant schools. Some Dad's Clubs have an online presence too – though it's tricky to Google a club if you don't know the name of it, but there's no harm in trying 'Dad's Clubs' and adding your town and going from there.

Some of the groups are an offshoot of established mother-and-baby services, and these are often promoted through the local health centre or GP. Family support groups and those specialising in helping one-parent families may prove useful too in helping you find a local club.

The NCT has also run some groups in the UK – www.nct.org.uk

The Fathers Network in Scotland can provide contacts for local clubs too: www.fathersnetwork.org.uk

---

Dad You Know?

Political Push for Professional Parenting

In line with the whole Dad's Clubs and parenting lessons push these days, politicians in the UK are investigating a national programme of baby bonding to be run at children's centres – with an emphasis on dads playing a bigger part.

After research suggested that there are gaps in levels of child development that only become apparent when children enter the education system, an All-Party Parliamentary Sure Start Group of MPs and peers recommended (in July 2013) a new scheme to make basic activities designed to help parents bond with their babies universally available.

Along with the appeal for courses to give parents advice on how to form secure attachments with their babies, the MPs also called for fathers to be treated as an 'equal party' alongside mothers at parent-and-toddler groups and similar services to encourage them to play a more active part in their children's upbringing.

The research that provoked the debate suggests that babies who form strong bonds with their parents in the first two years of their life are less likely to fail at school, become involved in crime and ultimately fail in their own relationships. Meanwhile, children whose parents do not interact with them – through talking, singing and story sessions, play and developmental games – are more likely to struggle at school.

Wisdom of Fathers

Join Da' Club

'It's useful for meeting different dads, ones I wouldn't have known from anywhere else, and discussing stuff. I found out about a park I didn't know of locally through one dad and we use it a lot now that Ben is toddling. The club also has lots of children's activities and toys like little cars for them to sit in, building bricks, play mats. It's nice and safe and we take turns in reading a story to a group too, which was a new experience.' Rob, father of Ben

WHAT CHECKS SHOULD I DO AROUND THE HOUSE?

You may have been through the tick list of things to do to baby-proof your home, but there are also a few regular checks worth doing to doubly ensure the safety of your whole family:

Smoke detectors

At times you're both likely to be exhausted, deprived of sleep and focused so much on the issues around your baby that things can slip your mind. Although there's no evidence that being new parents puts your home at greater risk of accidents like fires starting, the fact is there are around 50,000 house fires in the UK each year. Do your dad bit by getting a smoke alarm fitted in your home to give you and your new family plenty of warning if a fire does break out – an extra few seconds can make a real difference. It's best to have at least two smoke alarms. Have a think about how you would escape a fire with your baby too.

Carbon monoxide detector

This is another peace-of-mind move that's simple and inexpensive and can save you from the unthinkable. Because carbon monoxide has no odour and taste it's undetectable to humans. You gas service provider should be able to help you ensure you can get a CO detector fitted easily enough.

Check the seat

If you're taking your baby out in the car give the seat fittings another check over. Make sure it's fitted as per the manufacturer's instructions and don't be tempted to turn the seat to face forward even though your baby is getting bigger. Because babies have large heads and still-developing neck muscles they're still very fragile, and a head-on car collision can lead to spinal injuries in a baby who's sitting facing forward as their head jerks on impact. The expert advice is to keep your child in a rear-facing car seat until the age of two – though be prepared to upsize the seat (as in buy a new one) before then as your baby grows.

PETS

SHOULD WE STILL HAVE PETS WHEN WE HAVE A BABY?

Most pets and babies get along smoothly – many dads can dig out a picture of themselves as babies with their arms lovingly locked around the neck of the docile family dog. But there are of course reports every now and again in the media of serious dog attacks involving babies or young children. These incidents are rare but receive a large amount of media coverage and can serve as a reminder to us all to take additional care when introducing a new dog to the family home – or your new baby to the home of your faithful hound.

First off, it's worth flagging up the plus points of having a pooch at home. Aside from the comfort, companionship, fun and security you and your partner may get from having a dog, research also shows that dogs and cats can boost your baby's health.

Studies from Kuopio University Hospital in Finland, published in the journal *Pediatrics* in 2013, revealed that babies who grow up in homes with a pet dog or cat are less likely to get sick than children who live pet-free. Previous research has also linked the presence of pets with a lower risk of allergies among babies – and possibly preventing childhood asthma. The Finnish study also found that babies who grew up in homes with pets were 44 per cent less likely to develop an ear infection and 29 per cent less likely to receive antibiotics, compared with pet-free babies.

Dad You Know?

Who Let The Dog In?

One survey of 1,000 expectant parents by pet shelter charity Dogs Trust (www.dogstrust.org.uk) found that nearly one in five (18 per cent) parents had been told by family, friends and health professionals to give up their dog before their baby arrived. Of course there's no need to do this, and to help new parents the Dogs Trust provides a New Baby factsheet.

WHAT SHOULD I DO TO KEEP MY BABY SAFE AROUND MY PET?

While most dogs and cats are pretty tolerant towards little humans, once your baby starts shifting around on their own it pays to be aware of some of the potential dangers and take a few precautions to keep your baby safe.

- **Be aware of jealousy:** It's not just new dads that experience envy when babies come along. Make sure you give

attention to your pet in the presence of your baby and not
just when the baby is asleep. Your pet needs to know that
the presence of the baby is a good sign.

- **Don't push them together:** Let your pet interact with your
  baby at its own pace – but always supervise them together.
  Never leave a baby alone with your pet, no matter how
  trustworthy you may think they are.
- **Reward good behaviour:** Help your dog to see the baby as
  a nice thing to be around. Give your dog treats and lots of
  praise when he behaves well around the baby.
- **Take them walking:** Make sure your dog has enough exercise and things to do – a bored dog with too much energy
  can get up to all sorts of mischief while you are busy with
  your new baby.
- **Naps without cats:** Keep pets – especially cats – out of the
  room your baby sleeps in, and never let a cat or dog share
  a bed with your baby. Cats don't usually get jealous, but
  they are attracted to the warmth of a baby's cot.
- **Get a net:** Use a cat net on the pram or pushchair when it
  is downstairs or in the garden. Even if you don't own a
  cat, neighbouring cats can be curious.
- **Shut the gate:** Invest in a safety gate to keep your pets
  and your children apart, at least some of the time. Stair
  gates can also help keep your baby away from animal
  foods and litter trays. Curious babies have been known to
  use a cat flap to escape into the garden too.
- **Get them in the zone:** If you can, get your dog used to
  staying in a safe place – with his bed and a toy or treat to
  chew – for short periods of time every day. There will be
  times when you'll be busy with the baby, so training
  Rover to be happy on his own for a short time is going to
  help him cope with the changes ahead.
- **Make walks work:** Have a think about how you can make
  dog walking as easy as possible if you're going to be
  taking it out while with your baby too. Using a baby
  carrier might be easier than taking a pram as it leaves you
  with your hands free to hold the dog's lead.

- **Toy with them:** Dogs love cuddly toys but can find it tricky to differentiate between their toys and the baby's – one tip from the Dogs Trust experts is to keep the dog's toys separate and perhaps smear a tiny blob of peanut butter on them.

WHAT ABOUT WHEN OUR TODDLER IS AROUND DOGS?

When your child is old enough to understand, set some vital rules for them on how they must interact with your or anyone else's pooch.

- Always keep your child well away from your dog's food bowl.
- Never let your child interrupt your dog's sleep or take away his toys.
- Never let your child shout in your dog's face or pull his tail.

Wisdom of Fathers

From Here To Mutternity

'We had three dogs before we had our first child and all three slept in our bedroom, with at least one of them sleeping on the bed. As this would not be practical once the baby arrived due to space limitations in the room, and not wanting a dog on the bed while the baby was feeding, we changed this sleeping pattern several months before the baby arrived. So we moved two of the dog beds to the landing outside of the bedroom, and stopped the one dog coming up on to the bed to sleep. We also did things like getting the dogs used to spending a little more time on their own in their beds with a nice bone, as when a baby arrives naturally you don't have as much time to spend with your dogs as you did before.

We also introduced baby items, such as a pram, Moses basket, toys, etc. into the house long before the baby arrived, so the dogs got used to them being around. Then, once our daughter was born, as soon as we got home with her we let the dogs come and say hello and investigate her, so they didn't feel left out at all. The last thing we would have wanted is for our dogs to feel brushed aside, and in turn be jealous of the new arrival and the problems that can bring. At all times we made an effort to keep them included with everything and not to forget to still give them as much attention as we could – they were after all there first and important members of the family.' Adam, father of Yasmin (three) and Isaac (five weeks) and owner of two dogs, Troy and Molly

HOW DO I HELP MY BABY DEVELOP AT EIGHT MONTHS?

Dads can easily encourage their babies to develop their co-ordination, strength, mobility and those little grey cells.

Go all soft

With your baby moving around by their own steam, a fun way to play with them and aid their development can be to turn a room of your house into a temporary soft play area. Grab cushions, pillows and throws from around your home and set up a playground of obstacles for your baby to crawl over and shuffle around. You're not only unleashing the inquisitive adventurer within them but you're helping their bones and muscles strengthen in the process too.

Bring out a book

Keep on reading to your baby whenever you get the chance – even if it's just reading out the write-ups from the sports pages of the newspaper. Help them engage with books too – reading aloud, showing them the pictures, getting them to turn the page. Books that make noises, feature 'touch' sensation pages or are full of animals always go down well with babies.

Surprise, surprise

Your baby's sense and reactions at this age can bring much merriment for the rest of the family – as well as some potential money-making comedy home videos. Toys like a jack-in-the-box at this age can be fun and stimulating for them – honestly – as they develop a sense of anticipation. When they're sitting up it's fun to play 'I'm going to get you!' games where you move towards them and shower them with hugs and tickles.

WHAT'S A GOOD WAY TO ENCOURAGE MY BABY TO CRAWL?

Here's another opportunity for you to impress peers, partners and grandparents with your little boy or girl by revealing a couple of little tricks that can help encourage them to start crawling if they haven't already.

- **Learn purchase power:** Baby clothes and smooth floors are a slippery combination. So, when your little one is rocking on all fours and seemingly keen to crawl but not quite there, take off their trousers so that they're just in their nappy. It means they can get some purchase – their skin 'grips' the floor and so they can start to move.
- **Give 'em a goal:** Get a colourful toy of theirs and place it just out of their reach when they're getting into the crawl mode. Make a big fuss of them when they come and get the toy. Don't then toss it across the room and shout fetch.
- **Set a course:** Just as road joggers like to go trail running for a new challenge so you should change the terrain a

little as your baby begins to master the crawling habit. Use pillows, sofa cushions, cardboard boxes and the like to create obstacle courses for them to negotiate. They'll improve their co-ordination as they do and find crawling more fun in the process.

Dad You Know?

Strained Relations

A 2013 study by relationship charity OnePlusOne found almost two-thirds of new parents have a concern about their relationship that did not exist before. Often parents are so worried about their new roles – either staying at home or being the main breadwinner – that they neglect each other and stop regarding themselves as romantic partners. Around 40 per cent of new mothers who expressed worries feared they were no longer sexually attractive to their partners. At the same time, more than a quarter of new fathers were worried their partner had stopped wanting to make love.

9 DAD OR ALIVE?

Child's Life: Weeks 33–36

WHAT'S OCCURRING WITH OUR BABY AT THIS STAGE?

You're not going to recall what you were doing at nine months old and nor will your baby – but if they could then a diary entry around this time might look something like:

'Another tough day at floor level but with half an eye on promotion to 'cruising' any time now. Solids are still making regular appearances on this great new 'Wean Me Plan' diet I'm following right now. It's playing havoc with my nappies though – fortunately Dad's on hand a lot when the major deposits need processing. Haven't quite got the hang of this 'word' thing just yet but it's not through want of trying.'

WHAT'S A NINE-MONTH-OLD KID INTO THESE DAYS?

Babies are mysterious creatures when it comes to timing so while some nine-month-old nippers will be crawling, bawling, babbling and similar such behaviour – others will go at a slower pace. Certainly puzzles and games that involve fitting shapes into other shapes can keep them out of mischief and more crucially sharpen their minds and improve their co-ordination. Swimming and bathtime water games will continue to fascinate them – the light reflecting off the water can be as attractive as anything else at that age. Along with developing their own distinctive 'voice' – mimicking some words or applying ones like 'choo-choo' to toy trains or using ones like 'juice' for food, babies will have other ways of communicating their needs to you at this age aside simply from crying.

Weird Things Babies Do

Go Ape About Faces

Researchers have discovered that six-month-old babies can tell the difference between individual humans or individual monkeys. But by nine months, while babies could still differentiate between human faces, they couldn't tell one monkey from another.

SHOULD I KIT MY BABY OUT WITH THEIR FIRST SHOES YET?

It's tempting isn't it? Those first few steps could be imminent. They may already be up and standing in that wobbly newborn foal way. Those mini baby Adidas trainers would look so cool on them too. But if you can resist the urge to start decking them out in proper shoes before they're even a year old, do so.

For starters their bones are still quite fragile and obviously growing – so cramping them in tight footwear could stop their toes developing naturally. It's usually advisable to stick to soft booties until they can start walking on their own. And even then try to let them walk around indoors shoeless as much as possible.

Barefoot is also best at this time because it'll help your baby's muscles and tendons develop and they'll find it easier to get a decent grip on the floor and aid their balance once they are up on their two feet.

When you do come to buy them their first shoes – once they're up and walking without too many 'oops' moments – take a few toe-saving tips along with you:

- **Take a drawing as a template of your child's feet:** Do an outline of each foot on to a sheet of paper to get an idea of the size you need. If you're going to a specialist shop you can get them measured – but good luck with that if it's a fidgety toddler with stranger anxiety.
- **Go for 'natural' materials for kids' shoes:** They let the feet breathe and they're less likely to create the conditions in which bacteria grow than plastic shoes. If you want to avoid having to ask for something to treat a 'fungal condition' at the chemist then get your kid into canvas sandals, cotton plimsoll-style or leather shoes when the time is right. Welly boots are of course the exception.
- **Measure up regularly:** That seemingly continuous growth spurt your child is on does of course include their feet. With this in mind it's worth getting their feet measured regularly – and especially once they're walking. Check that their shoes aren't leaving marks on their feet where they're getting too tight. Also ditch any socks they may have grown out of or have lost their shape. A good children's shoe shop will always ask to measure a little one's feet and not ask you what size they are.
- **Do some papa pedicure:** Be sure to dry between your baby's toes after bathtime and if needs be trim their toenails straight across to stop them in-growing.

Dad You Know?

Beauty in the Eye of the Baby Holder ...

Around one in five new parents secretly believes their baby is ugly. A pool of 1,000 mums and dads revealed that 18 per cent of new mothers and fathers owned up to being privately disappointed with the looks of their new arrivals. But 82 per cent said their new baby was the most beautiful thing they had ever seen.

HOW DOES OUR BABY GROW?

Not as strange a question as it may sound. You may be fully familiar with the intricacies of baby growth and the new parent phenomena of the 'centiles'. You may have been plotting the graph yourself on your baby's own chart – provided as part of their personal record around the time of their birth as a means of tracking your child's progress. But if you haven't, here's a heads-up.

Boy and girl babies have different 'centile' charts because boys are usually heavier and taller at this stage than girls and their growth path is slightly different. In the baby's home health record book there's a red line for the average size running through the centre of the page – and two blue outer lines either side of it.

The idea is for the parents to regularly weigh and measure their baby. The book is designed to cover the first couple of years and by drawing a line from each measurement point you plot the progress of your own child against the averages. In the event of you noting a drop beneath the lower centile – showing a reduction in weight or slowing in your baby's growth – it should be pointed out to your GP or health visitor.

—— *Wisdom of Fathers* ——

Growing Pains

'Our biggest health concern so far has been around feeding. Our baby doesn't drink the quantities that she should be and as a result has dropped two centiles – also she's had thrush and reflux, so we thought this was the cause but we're now waiting to see a paediatrician in case the cause is something else.' Sunil, father of Riya

HOW CAN I START SAVING FOR MY KID'S FUTURE?

Possibly the last thing you want to think about right now is another major outlay of cash. But if you want to avoid being hit with demands for dosh with menaces from your baby when they reach their teens and want to go off to university it's worth sparing a moment to consider some savings options.

One possible venture is a Junior ISA. Until 2011 newborns were entitled to a payment designed to help parents start up a Child Trust Fund. Since that date the payments have been scrapped and now parents are advised to consider investing any money they want to put away for their child into a Junior Individual Savings Account (JISA).

These JISAs are available in both cash and stocks and shares types – the idea is that you choose the one you want and deposit funds as and when you can – it can come in handy if people want to give you money as a gift for your baby's birthday too. Anyone can pay money into a JISA – but the total amount deposited can't go over £3,720 in a tax year (as at August 2013).

The money can't be withdrawn until your child is 18. The cash JISA means you don't pay tax on interest on the cash you save. With the stocks and shares JISA your cash is invested and you won't pay tax on any capital growth or dividends you receive.

Although you can get the information from the www.gov.uk website you actually set up the JISA yourself with a bank, building society, credit union or stockbroker.

AM I REALLY MAKING A DIFFERENCE AS A DAD?

Just because you're a few months down the line in the job of dad doesn't mean you've mastered it by any means and it certainly doesn't mean you're going to be totally at ease with your new-found role in life. Many men will question their function as fathers during various points in the journey. Certainly at this stage when your baby is still so dependent and bonded with its mother you could find yourself wondering what influence if any you're really having in their life.

Well, as ever, there's some handy research out there, which may put your troubled mind at rest.

In a review of 36 different studies by a research team at the University of Connecticut psychologists found that a father's love contributes as much – and sometimes more – to the development of their child as a mother's love does.

The focus of the studies was on the power and effects of parental rejection and acceptance and how they shape the personality of our children. When it comes to the effect of a dad's love the study results suggest that while children and adults often experience more or less the same level of acceptance or rejection from each parent, the influence of one parent's rejection – often a dad's – can be much greater than the other's.

A separate group of psychologists – working on a mouthful of a programme called the International Father Acceptance Rejection Project – suggests that this may be because children hold fathers in higher esteem, perceiving Dad as having more power or prestige and so possibly see him as having more influence in their life than their mother. (No doubt plenty of mums would like to give the International Father Acceptance Rejection Project a volley of feedback on that particular point.) The research does conclude that fatherly love is critical to a person's development – and crucial to reducing the risk of behaviour problems and maladjustment as the child gets older.

Weird Things Babies Do

Change their Eye Colour

The colour pigment in the main tissue of the baby's eyes can take up to a year to develop, which is why in many cases babies are born with blue eyes – regardless of their genetics. By around nine months the melanin is activated by your baby's genetics and their 'natural' eye colour – blue, brown, hazel, green or whatever – becomes established.

HOW DO I FIND THE TIME TO BE A DAD?

While many modern workplaces are clued up as to the requirements of families these days, it doesn't mean that all new families are happily managing to strike that perfect balance between home life and work. For most of us that time when our baby comes along can create a whole load of new challenges and additional pressures that can affect our work life and vice versa.

Sleep deprivation can have a devastating toll on your energy levels and ability to function beyond the basics some days – no wonder it's used as a form of torture. The demands of having an extra mouth to feed can also increase the pressure levels too. There's a huge additional requirement for you as a breadwinner – quite possibly the chief one – to keep hold of your job and if possible make it pay more, while also enabling you more time to spend with your new family. It's nigh on impossible to find that happy medium of course.

First off, recognising that you're going to be pulled around by these competing demands is one big step towards dealing with them and achieving the best balance you can. Talk with your partner – all the time – about how the needs of work and family are affecting you. Don't be tempted to avoid the subject or conceal your concerns for fear of putting any burden upon your partner. Your own health, well-being, energy and strength are most vital to your partner and your baby right now – anything that's hampering your ability to be a supportive father right now needs to be discussed so that you can find positive, proactive ways of dealing with any problems.

Dad You Know?

Take a Sickie!

Research shows that few fathers get to spend a great deal of time alone with their child. A survey by the Australian Institute of Family Studies found that on weekdays children may spend as little as half an hour alone with their fathers. Even at weekends, children spend only a relatively small number of hours with their father when their mother isn't there – varying from 0.8 hours a day for infants to 1.4 hours for two to three year olds.

The real shame is that those dads who do get to spend more time with their kids have been recorded as having significantly improved relationships with their children. According to the experts – such as Dr Graeme Russell, associate professor of psychology and author of *First-Time Father* – this is partly because those dads who do spend more time with their baby develop a stronger understanding of their needs and build a close connection through sharing activities together.

Discover How Much Time you Really Have with your Baby ...

Some new dads will even look at doing a time 'audit' – possibly at the behest of their partners – to help prioritise their time better. For those spreadsheet lovers among you this can be done by setting up a Microsoft Excel plan of your average working week. For the non-geeks get a pen and paper when you have five minutes and do this:

- Across the top of the page plot the days of the week from Monday through to Sunday.
- In the left-hand, first column break the day down into hours – from when your baby first wakes right through until when you go to bed.
- Draw horizontal and vertical lines on the page so you have a grid that divides each day up into hours.
- Now start to colour in each hour using a different shade for: work time, commute time, home time, any specific time you get with your baby alone (when your partner's out or napping) and time you get together with just your partner. You may want to add another colour for time spent with friends and other family.

Once you've done that check out any surprises – such as there's much more commute time on some days or you spend absolutely no time alone with your partner.

Look for any areas where you might be able to make some changes to your working week to win back some more time for yourself.

This kind of thing often serves as a means of underlining what you already know – but it can also help you focus more on making priorities, such as trying to get more flexi-time from work or arranging childcare so that you and your partner can leave the house at least once a week!

Wisdom of Fathers

Old Father Time

'I think that being a parent means feeling guilty. Most of the time, I spend more time with Elias than most dads I know spend with their kids. When I'm not with him, I wish I was, but when I am with him I sometimes wish I could have a break! Overall I think I get a good deal – I don't see that I should take any less responsibility for childcare than Fleur does.' Mike, father of Elias

HOW CAN I SWITCH FROM WORK TO FAMILY TIME?

It may seem like a pretty obvious thing to be able to do but it can be tough making that separation between the office and your role as a new father. It's all too easy to bring work home or have one eye on business and the other on Baby. If you want to devote all your attention to your little one a few useful ways of getting work to work better for you could be to:

- **Do homework at nap time:** If you're going to have to work from home at times try and schedule it around your baby's nap time or feed time with his or her mum.
- **Switch to silent:** Avoid taking calls or leave the answerphone on during those high-activity periods when you want a bit of quality time with your baby, like bathtime, feeds and bedtime.
- **Split the chores:** If you're both working now you may want to look at setting up a pattern of sharing the baby care – if you're more of a 'mornings person' than your partner or just have more time first thing then you could split the work-load.

- **Call time on the job:** Get into the habit of having a 'switch off' time when you get home from work. This could be a ritual where you get home, give your baby a big kiss, change clothes, switch off the phone and then catch up on your baby and partner's day – share your experiences of the day – and spend time playing with, bathing or feeding your baby.

Wisdom of Fathers

Work–Life Balance

'Because I'm working full-time in removals it's a very demanding job with some irregular hours and a reliance on good traffic for me to get home some days in time to spend time with Charlie. I'm often home late, tired, hungry and not great company to be honest. I get more time with him in the morning and sometimes I wake up early and wait until he's awake to give him a feed, change him and just get some time together.' Sam, father of Charlie at 11 months

HOW CAN I HELP MY NINE MONTH OLD DEVELOP RIGHT NOW?

A few useful little challenges to run by your baby right now may add to your armoury of 'fun things Baby does with Dad' as well as boost their own skill set. (Sorry, I won't use 'skill set' to describe how a baby does stuff again.)

Balloon batting

Ah, the simple toys are often the most fun ... at least until your child is old enough to appreciate the whole interactive gaming experience that comes with a Nintendo DS. A balloon really can prove to be a useful tool for training hand–eye co-ordination. Just moving the balloon from side to side as they're lying on the floor or sitting up and encouraging your little one to hit or kick it. They're developing reactions and if you dangle the balloon so that it moves when they hit it you'll soon see how they master 'anticipation' of the balloon's return after they hit it.

Get in the box!

What a great use of the box that the new car seat/buggy/crib/TV came in. At nine months he or she will definitely be into setting up camp in an empty box. Crawling in and out of a box on its side or simply sitting in it and peeking out (cut some playhouse windows in the side before you let them loose on it) will get many a baby positively peeing themselves with excitement, unfortunately. The baby development experts will tell you this is great for enhancing a baby's spatial relations. If they could, the baby would tell you it's just a bit of a laugh really.

Point and focus

When sharing books, encourage your baby to move their eyes around the page and to point out what they want by you pointing at different pictures on the pages you read to them. Your baby might already have a favourite book at this stage – don't miss an opportunity to introduce new books to them all the time. You can get fabric books and even ones they can play in the bath with.

Bits of the body

This is a double whammy of increasing your baby's familiarity with their body parts and making the chore of getting them dressed that little bit more fun too. Telling them you're putting the sock on their foot – or the vest over their tummy – giving each body part a tickle as your say it. A variation on this theme involves getting a water pistol or squirt toy at bathtime and using it to squirt water at the body part they point to when you ask them (not ideal for 'eye' but 'tummy' is a safe target). It'll increase their language awareness and the accuracy of your aim in the process.

Assorted stuff

The compulsion to organise, file away and sort stuff out becomes quite strong around this age. You may already notice them sorting their toys into specific piles or groups. You can encourage it with simple toys like putting balls into plastic cups or even using a Yorkshire pudding tray as the base for sorting objects into – just avoid small stuff that they could swallow.

Wisdom of Fathers

Developing Solution

'Childhood isn't a rat race and there's really no need to push your baby to do stuff that others are supposedly doing. My wife would get upset that Tyler wasn't as active or didn't seem as interested in toys as some of the children at her one o'clock club. But we've since realised it's not a uniform thing – children develop at their own rate, and he's toddling around now, into everything and absolutely fine.'
Paul, father of Tyler (two) and Niamh (four months)

WHAT'S NORMAL SLEEP FOR NINE MONTHS?

Well, babies being the way they are – human – means nothing is totally normal, but they should be sleeping through the night by now with no need for night feeds. If they're not, you might want to consider some 'sleep training' to help them learn to cope without milk feeds during the night. Some will even clock up a decent 12 hours' worth of kip at this stage – in preparation for their teenage years possibly. BUT ... and as you probably realise by now there's always a 'but' with babies ... if they're teething or going through a hunger-inducing growth spurt don't be surprised if you're still subject to being jolted awake in the wee hours by your infant's wails.

You can reduce the likelihood of them waking from hunger by giving them a small snack or milky drink after their evening meal but before bedtime.

SHOULD OUR BABY BE WATCHING TV?

Definitely one to spark debate on the parenting websites, young children and TV viewing is – unsurprisingly – a well-researched topic. The most recent in-depth investigation carried out by the American Academy of Pediatrics recommends no TV for children under the age of two – and only half an hour a day for those over two.

Babies don't have much time for the American Academy of whatever – they do however find the motion, colour, sound and characters of most childish TV thoroughly engaging. (Though even they will draw a line at *Big Brother*.) The US experts warn that even 'passive' exposure to television can harm a baby's language development – that's adults watching TV with their baby nearby.

In reality, TV will act as a 'babysitter' for most kids at some time or another. With the best will in the world mums and dads will resort to plonking their toddler in front of CBeebies or Channel 5's *Milkshake!* shows while they desperately try to sort out an aspect of their life that isn't baby-related.

It's true that when the TV is on in a room there's a lot less of the 'talk time' the experts insist is vital to child development. Perhaps one of the other factors to consider when rationing your baby's TV exposure is overstimulation. Cramming too much stimulating entertainment into a baby's day can overload them and there is research that says this can trigger restlessness, sleep problems and moodiness.

- Avoid leaving your baby alone watching TV if you can – if you're going to watch it do it together.
- Minimise the time they spend in front of the box – whenever possible read to them or stick to simple toys that don't require batteries or charging.
- Switch the TV off when no one's watching it. If there is anything in that American research into passive TV viewing it's perhaps worth preventing it becoming an issue for your little one.

Wisdom of Fathers

Building the Bond

'Bonding hasn't been much of a problem as she's stuck to me like a koala bear. I can only suggest lots of cuddles, talking to her using normal voices (which is very important for speech development), lots of eye contact and playing with her regularly even if it is at 2am.' Chris, father of Milly, Meredith and Nellie

WHAT THE BLOODY HELL IS BABY YOGA?

Ah, the next step on from the aforementioned 'out there' parent–baby bond session that is baby massage is the equally odd, but just as relaxing for all involved, baby yoga. To be fair it's not really asking much of your baby this one – they won't be clad in lycra and forced to stretch themselves in the lotus position.

It's a gentle series of positions that parent and baby adopt – under the guidance of a tutor – which, a lot like baby massage, is said to enhance their communication and confidence. Some practitioners will bang on about its digestive and sleep benefits too. New mums often find it a useful form of postnatal de-stressing that can also iron out some of their birth aches and pains around the pelvic floor and lower back. Dads just find it a pretty chilling way to hang out with their baby and take their mind off stuff for a while ... sorry I mean of course they find it a worthwhile, therapeutic, flexibility-boosting and de-stressing bonding session.

HOW MUCH SHOULD MY NINE MONTH OLD BE EATING?

From around nine months onwards babies will be finding out how they fit into the family meal schedule. They're ideally chomping through three chopped-up meals a day and still washing it all down with around 600 ml (1 pt) of breast milk or formula – plus fruit snacks.

If you're vegetarians and looking to raise your baby as one then it's easy to ensure your baby gets a balanced diet. If you're eating animal by-products and including them in your baby's diet – such as milk, cheese and eggs – you'll be ensuring that they do get the calcium and protein they need for development.

HOW DO WE GET OUR KID TO EAT ANY VEGETABLES?

It seems like you're never too young to be fussy. An infant can try a food up to 20 times before deciding whether they like it or not – so don't be too alarmed if they're flatly refusing those cucumber sticks at first. Depending on their age there are some useful – sneaky – ways of getting fruit and vegetables into your child's diet.

- Mix fruit – fresh or tinned – in with yoghurts or *fromage frais* to disguise the taste.
- Mash up vegetables and mix them with rice or mashed potatoes.

- Purée them and mix with a pasta sauce.
- Try them with sweet potato and carrots – they're a little sweeter tasting than some green vegetables.
- Mix fruits and vegetables together – you may not be able to stomach it but babies have no issues as to what food should accompany other ones.
- Make a point of eating vegetables in front of your baby – go on Dad, you know you love 'em ... Do it with over-acted glee and he or she may be won over to give those sprouts a try.

Also, as they get more used to solids, be sure to give them beans and other non-dairy sources of protein, including soya, pulses, nuts and seeds. Energy-rich foods such as avocado, banana and hummus are good for growing babies. It's not a good idea to give whole nuts to babies as they're a choking hazard – try them with smooth nut butter instead. Take note: when introducing nuts to a child's diet you may want to consult a nutrition specialist – especially if you have a family history of allergies.

10

STAY-AT-HOME DAD

Child's Life: Weeks 37–40

WHAT'S HAPPENING WITH OUR BABY'S DEVELOPMENT AT 10 MONTHS?

Aside from the more obvious stuff – like the fact that your baby will be learning more and more each day and that by constantly talking to them you can be developing their communication skills – your baby will be undergoing a lot more subtle changes at this time. As they become more aware so they'll start developing responses that you'll be very familiar with – don't be surprised if they:

- Get alarmed or upset by surprises – the phone ringing, dog barking, doorbell going, etc. can all trigger #startled-face in your nipper.
- Decide that now's the time to crawl – or, if they're crawling already, that now's the time to stand up. If already standing, then walking and … well, you get the idea.
- Show a preferred hand for picking things up.
- Develop a vocabulary that could be bulging beyond 'mama', 'dada' and 'bye-bye', depending on how they're developing to 'dog,' 'cat' or most likely 'no!'
- Become more stubborn or persistent – depending on how

194

you interpret it – when it comes to doing things they want to do.

- Have problems with feeds if they're focused on a particular toy or activity.

CAN I ARRANGE MORE FLEXIBLE WORKING?

Around now, your partner will probably be making final decisions about a return to work. This decision impacts immensely on all three of you and it will involve tough choices made with the head, not just the heart. It's worth looking into all of the options for you both – while one of you may earn more, another may have more flexibility in the workplace.

Anyone can ask their employer to work flexibly and employees who care for a child have the legal right to ask for flexible working ... but you have to fit certain criteria for flexible working (to make a statutory request) and your employer doesn't have to agree to the request.

Often new dads are wary of doing this because of the stigma that's seemingly attached in some workplaces. You might be concerned that you'll be seen as a slacker or just fear that you'll get overlooked for projects or promotion if you're seen as bit of a 'part-timer'. Attitudes are changing though and many companies realise that in order to retain the best people they at least have to meet those who request more flexible working hours half way.

If you've sounded out your boss or colleagues or your HR department and think that it could work for you and your firm then the recommended way to go about it is to put in a formal request.

You put your application in writing to your employer requesting a meeting within 28 days to discuss it. Explain why you're requesting a flexible working pattern, explain when you want it to start and let them know how you plan to stop it having a disastrous effect upon the company ...

You'll need to put together a business case that sells the idea to your boss – explaining how you'll ensure it's going to work out, how you'll be so much better at your job when you've actually had some sleep and how it will impact on your colleagues. (You can sound out your workmates too ahead of the meeting if you want to gauge their thoughts too.)

Your employer should let you know within 14 days of the meeting of their decision, and if they agree to flexible working they should give you a new contract. But they can refuse it for such reasons as the 'extra costs damaging the business' or 'flexible working will have an effect on quality and performance'. You employer must meet with you to discuss this. There are chances to appeal decisions and you can find out the exact legal situation at www.gov.uk

SHOULD I TAKE OVER RAISING OUR BABY?

It's possible this topic has come up already since you became a new dad – or even before you did. Now that you've spent a little time at home with your baby – and then left them behind to head out to work – it's possible your feelings may have changed. You won't be the only dad experiencing this.

Some reports put the number of men staying at home to look after children at around 227,000 in the UK. Other studies suggest that one in seven fathers now adopt the 'primary caregiving role'. But there's much debate as to the validity of the data used to collate these figures. The first one is based upon employment statistics and not a direct survey of actual stay-at-home dads. According to Gideon Burrows, the author of *Men Can Do It!*, which examines how childcare is shared in the UK, the figure is more likely to be around 57,000 men.

Whatever it is, you could be forgiven for thinking that it's just not the done thing for dads to be at home with their baby – unless they can't afford not to be there. The media representation of stay-at-home dads isn't the most reassuring, according to Dr Abigail Locke, a reader in applied social psychology at the University of Huddersfield who undertook analysis on the depiction of fathers and parenting in the media.

'I found very few examples of it being a "choice" for men – it was always driven by finances. There was a common equality aspect – that because the mum earns more, it was the obvious choice. More negative press focused on it as emasculating and on the stigma attached,' explains Locke.

Some typical headlines from 2013 on the topic of stay-at-home dads included: 'I Was So Proud to be a Stay-at-Home Dad. Now I Fear it's Harmed my Daughter ...' and 'Why Being a Stay-at-Home Dad is the Quickest Way to Kill your Sex Life ...'

You get the gist. But in reality plenty of dads who take the plunge, be it through choice or necessity, report having a wonderful experience on the whole, with moments of boredom, tension, anxiety and more boredom thrown in. Pretty much the same as most mothers to be honest.

The idea of being a 'full-time father' may strike you as being totally nuts. Alternatively, if you enjoyed your role during paternity leave and at weekends it may be something you want to investigate some more.

It's true that one of the key reasons why many new dads become stay-at-home ones is financial. When your wife or partner returns to work after the birth, she could be in a position where she earns enough to keep the home ticking over while almost all your income would be swallowed up by childcare costs. So in that instance many dads 'opt' to stay at home.

There are of course pros and cons to becoming a stay-at-home dad.

Pros of being a stay-at-home dad:

- The opportunity to watch your child grow, to shape their personality and be much more involved in their day-to-day life.
- Being there for those landmark moments.
- Having more time by exchanging the trials and tribulations of daily commutes for a life at home.

- The satisfaction of doing a challenging and hugely rewarding job.
- Changes in stress levels as a full-time father versus full-time employee.
- Time to pursue other interests (don't get too carried away at the thought of this though).

Cons of being a stay-at-home dad:

- Change in status – some men find it a struggle since they equate their job with who they are and consider themselves 'jobless' in the eyes of others. Are you ready to introduce yourself as a 'stay-at-home dad' when asked what you do for a living?
- Kiss goodbye to the company perks and social whirl of work life.
- Drop in income.
- DROP IN INCOME. (That includes pensions, paid holiday and sick leave.)
- Mental stagnation and feelings of isolation – staying in the house all day and attempting to hold high-brow chats with a baby will prove draining at times. You'll soon see why dads who go out to work get such a warm welcome when they come home in the evening.

HOW CAN I SEE IF LIFE AS A STAY-AT-HOME DAD IS FOR ME?

Some dads give it a trial run during a week's holiday to see if they can hack it. Others have to do it and struggle to cope, bemoaning everything until they finally return to the world of paid work. It's not for everyone. But if you are taking over the childcare from your partner, a few starting points to consider are:

- **Make it your own:** Try to establish your own routine rather than trying to do exactly as your partner has. Your baby will be set in their own routine now which will dictate how you run the show – but make it your own role by gradually building up your own social interactions and daily, weekly and even long-term plans.

- **Share the load:** If your partner is giving up her role she may well feel left out at first especially. Keep her involved, make time during the day to contact each other and be sure to fill her in on what you and your baby have been up to during the day.
- **Gang up:** Do investigate joining a Dad's Club (see Chapter 8) and make an effort to get to know other parents. Their support can prove to be invaluable at times.

Wisdom of Fathers

Stay-at-Home Dads

'I became a full-time, stay-at-home dad in a small first-floor flat with no garden. I thought it would be a great idea – but I struggled from the off. Sleep is everything and if you're not recharging the batteries then you can't function normally.' Lee Gale, father of two boys

'I gave up work four years ago to look after our son while my wife continued in her HR job. Now I stay at home with both our children. I combined it with some copywriting, which I'd done before and managed to get some freelance work in. It's not easy because no matter how much you try to get your child into a routine they seem determined to drag you away from any chance you have of working. I found the oddest part of it all was dealing with groups of mums – some of whom I think thought I was hitting on them when to be honest I would just be passing the time of day while taking Noah to the park.' Chester, father of Noah and Abi

SHOULD I HELP OUT WITH CHILDCARE BY WORKING FROM HOME?

It's not as easy as it sounds when you've got a baby or toddler to attend to. Right now your baby demands almost constant attention to the point where, some days, you may come home from work and your partner's barely had a chance to take a pee let alone do anything else. In the future you may be able to do some 'tele-working' but don't expect to be able to switch from a nine-to-five to a full-time dad's life and still be able to meet deadlines or work demands.

Dad You Know?

Working From Home

According to data from the Office of National Statistics perhaps as many as a fifth of the UK workforce now do a significant amount of their work from home – many in an attempt to juggle earning a crust with raising a child. If you're going to give it a go bear in mind a few useful pointers:

- **Fit around feeds:** If you're going to have to make calls or devote specific times of the day to tasks, schedule these for times when you're sure you're going to have some help with the childcare.

- **Get a secure line:** If you're using a second phone on the same line try to make sure the phone is out of the reach of your child. Sod's Law dictates that the moment you receive that important call from the boss will be the first time your child decides to pick up that ringing thing in the corner and burble into it like daddy does ...

- **Discipline yourself:** Treat work from home like being in the office. Focus on the job you need to do and don't be tempted into doing a bit of DIY or watching the TV unless you've scheduled it into your day.

Even though your baby may still be napping a couple of times a day, when they're asleep there will be other house management chores to be done – including putting away the weekly shopping you just bought, cleaning, cooking and more than anything dealing with the spontaneous demands of a toddler.

WILL MY PARTNER GOING BACK TO WORK AFFECT OUR BABY?

The issue of mums returning to work and the impact it may or may not have upon their baby is another hot topic for message board debate. Every year it seems a different set of research is presented and reported upon that sways the argument one way or another. The most recent evidence seems to suggest that there is no negative impact on a child's educational attainment if mum goes back to their job within 18 months of giving birth.

This apparently is thanks to you, Dad! Researchers Paul Gregg, professor of economics at Bristol University, and Elizabeth Washbrook, a student at Oxford, suggest that kids fare fine when mum returns to work due to a 'higher level of involvement in playing with, reading to and singing to their children on the part of the father, as well as the mother sacrificing more leisure time to compensate for her absence.'

The studies were based on the outcomes of 9,000 babies tracked through their schooling in the UK since the 1990s. The study also concluded that if a mother left her child in the care of friends and relatives, often grandparents, then the children subsequently went on to do a little less well at school.

WHAT WILL RETURNING TO WORK BE LIKE FOR MY PARTNER?

Some new mums welcome the chance to get stuck back into their career – many will have returned to work just a few months after their baby arrived – either through choice or necessity. Other mums hate it but have to persist with working while leaving their baby with a carer. Most make changes to their working day to spend as much time as they can with their child. Some go back to work, struggle with the separation or childcare arrangements and decide to quit and become 'full-time' mums – for want of a better term. One common issue for new mums surrounds the relationship they have with their employer after their baby comes along – and can sometimes begin during their pregnancy.

Dad You Know?

Workplace Woes

A 2013 study of 1,975 women carried out by a legal firm called Slater and Gordon found that just over a third of new mums experienced career setbacks that they put down to having had children.

In the study 35 per cent of the mothers said their workplace was not supportive of their situation when they were pregnant and 31 per cent felt they were not well treated by their employer while on maternity leave.

Around a quarter of new mums also said they had felt under pressure to return to work earlier than they wanted to. Once back in the workplace, almost half of the women questioned said they felt they had been overlooked for a promotion or thought their chances of career progression had been halted since becoming a mother.

Although pregnant and new mums are protected against discrimination in work that doesn't mean it doesn't go on. The same survey found that 51 per cent of new mums thought the attitudes of colleagues and their bosses towards them changed once they had announced their pregnancy – 18 per cent of new mums felt demoted and 35 per cent had had responsibility taken off them.

But the bulk of those who felt aggrieved by the way they'd been treated resisted making a formal complaint about unfair treatment – many of them because they 'did not want to rock the boat'.

So there's a chance your partner will not only be struggling with feelings of separation and even guilt about returning to work and leaving your baby with a carer – but she also could be having a pretty rough time of it when she's back at the coal-face too.

Although many companies and businesses are much better than they ever have been in accommodating the needs of working mums, not all are. If you're able to help her to find ways of making flexible working an option for either of you it's worth pursuing at this stage.

- Help ease the transition by getting childcare in place a week or so before she goes back to work, if it's financially feasible. It'll give you all a chance to set into place the morning routine, iron out any problems and ease her mind at little.
- Are there ways that your wife or partner can check in with the carer and even see your baby – maybe set up Skype so that your carer can use it – or just make sure that both mum and carer have each other's phone numbers? Getting the childminder to send pics to you both at work during the day can be a nice touch.
- If you're the first one home at the end of the working day can you prepare things so that Mum has some one-to-one time with the baby that's not stressful? Maybe sort out some chores or the meals so that Mum can do bathtime or a bedtime read.
- Your babysitter could take pictures (with her phone) of your baby during outings then send them to you both so you can see what they're up to.
- Ask your childminder to keep a note of any landmark moments or illness or special events during their day together and to fill you in on them at the end of the day.
- When you're both back at work again one of the toughest parts of the process is adjusting to how little time you'll both have with your baby – especially if they're likely to be going to bed early in the evening. That

change can be tougher on mum if she's had a long or extended maternity leave where she's spent her entire day with your baby.

CAN I STILL GET LEAVE TO LOOK AFTER MY BABY?

From March 2013 parents have been entitled to take up to 18 weeks' unpaid parental leave (an increase from the previous entitlement of 13 weeks). If you've not investigated this already it may be worth considering as your child is about to have another round of vaccinations, which will require a trip to the GP.

Parental leave is designed to cover childcare problems and attending appointments with children – or simply taking time off to spend with your kid/s. To qualify for the right the employee must have at least one year's continuous service and have, or expect to have, responsibility for a child. It's available for parents of children up to five years old. The right remains limited to a maximum of four weeks per year (unless agreed otherwise) and should be taken in blocks of at least a week.

This increase in parental leave time – the result of a European directive – is the first of a number of other changes planned by the government which intends to provide greater flexibility for parents. Proposals due to come in during 2015 are currently under consultation and include an extended right to request flexible working and a scheme of shared parental leave which, despite its name, is different to the 'parental leave' explained above. 'Shared parental leave' is designed to effectively allow parents to share the statutory maternity leave and pay that is currently available only to mothers (and with equivalent provisions in respect of adoptions).

Weird Things Babies Do

Guilt Trips

Dropping off Baby first thing in the morning or collecting them in the evening can trigger tears – on the part of both the baby and parent at times. While it isn't a deliberate manipulative ploy by your baby to tug on the heart-strings – it's possibly that they pick up on and react to their parent's anxiety. There's also an element of 'stranger' worry that can come into play when Mum hands Baby over to the childminder, which can also set them off. Even weirder is how some babies will burst into tears when they see Mum or Dad again at the end of their day with the childminder. It's possible that this is a relief reaction on their part – a way of them relaxing now Mum or Dad is here. Some parents get worried that their baby isn't happy but almost every childminder will tell you (rightly) that your baby is fine a few minutes after you've gone off to work and they're engaged in something else.

CAN MY STRUGGLING WITH FATHERHOOD AFFECT OUR BABY?

The memories of your child's actual birth could be fading already – such has been the last action-packed 10 months. You may have glanced at the section on postnatal depression a few months back or skipped past it because it didn't seem to apply to you. The likelihood is it won't be an issue for you – statistically at least.

But with possible changes in your family life now with your partner returned to work or an overhaul of how you're balancing work and Baby there's every chance anxiety, worry and depression could occur. While you may be trying your best to deal with demands placed upon you, dads who are suffering from depression can unwittingly have a negative effect on their child's development too.

US researchers have found that the fathers of nine month olds are twice as likely as other men their age to show symptoms of major depression. The same studies – presented to the American Psychiatric Association – found that depressed dads will read less to their kids and incidentally limit their child's vocabulary. Around 10 per cent of dads with babies around 9 to 10 months old showed symptoms of clinical depression.

Oxford University studies also found that a father's depression when a child is a baby can be linked to psychiatric disorders in children when they reach infant school. The researchers insist that a baby's ability to absorb the feelings around them can have a knock-on effect in later life if their dad is suffering from depression. The children of depressed fathers were nearly twice as likely to be defiant, disobedient and hostile, and the experts conclude that dads who struggle to adjust to parenthood should seek professional help. (See information about PND in Chapter 4.)

HOW DO I TEACH A BABY RIGHT FROM WRONG?

First off, for all those who knock dads for often being the 'good cop' or 'fun dad' it should be pointed out that a father who's full of fun and games is a major plus for the development of a child. That's not just the view of laugh-a-minute lads with kids either.

The best move you can make at this stage is to follow all the child-proofing tips (see Chapter 7) to not only reduce the risk of your child inadvertently doing mischief but also to cut down on the amount of times you're going to have to say 'No!' – therefore not wearing out the word, so to speak.

You and your partner should work on a few ground rules that you'll want your baby to follow, for example not eating on the sofa, or crawling/walking in the kitchen. It's useful to get into the habit of agreeing rules with your partner – and babysitters or grandparents – so that there's some consistency. It'll serve you well as your baby gets older, honestly.

Bear in mind of course that your baby will learn through trial, error and no end of exploration, so don't resort to making everything off limits, just be prepared to explain why – when they're old enough to understand – the cat litter tray isn't a great place to play.

As they grow beyond their first year, tips that have worked for dads trying to do discipline without being too Victorian include:

Combine words and actions

Saying 'no' alone won't work every time, especially in the early days. You'll need to follow up the statement with an act, such as physically removing your baby from the spot they're in. In the event of them reacting with a tantrum you may find taking them to another part of the house – changing the setting and giving them different distractions – will temper things quickly.

Giveth and taketh away

If you're going to have to say 'no,' try to follow it up with a positive, maybe providing a safer alternative place to play or toy to play with than the fork/fireguard/cat that they're grasping.

Get down to their level

With frustration and the struggle to communicate what they want often being the root cause of a lot of tantrums, try to always get down to their level when there's any tension. Meet them eye to eye and listen to what they're trying to say.

Stick to your guns

Avoid wavering over any disciplinary issues in favour of an easy life. Say no and stick to it. Babies and toddlers will suss out any indecision on your part and do their best to nudge you into giving in to them – usually through a persuasive argument based upon screaming loudly.

Pick your battles

Sometimes you'll find that taking a fun approach to laying down the law – making up silly songs or acting the fool – can take some of the upset out of an argument you're having with your little one. This means that when you do have to be serious and sharp with them – such as when something they're doing could be dangerous – you'll get their attention and the desired behaviour a lot quicker.

Lead the way

Babies are brilliant mimics. Their absorbent little brains soak up all we teach them – much of which we don't even realise we're passing on at the time. As a result one of the best ways of disciplining your kid is by simply giving them good examples of the best ways to behave. By seeing you using 'please' and 'thank you', by seeing you apologise when you make an error or swear in front of them or get annoyed, by seeing you explain why something's wrong they'll pick up good behaviour a whole lot quicker.

Be a cool dad

One of the toughest parts of the whole disciplining process is disciplining yourself to stay cool in the face of broken household items or mistakes made by your little one as they learn their way. Taking time to explain why something is wrong will give your child a much better chance of getting things right than flying off the handle. While there's a time and place for punishments like 'naughty steps' and 'time out' they're not really much use at this age. Keep calm and try to correct them instead of admonishing them.

Wisdom of Fathers

Raising girls

'Be persistent, always. Try to answer every question they ask you, which being girls is a lot. It can feel like herding cats but you'll always get there in the end. Make sure they know they can come to you and discuss anything, even if it's something embarrassing or involves trouble. Talk through things rather than tell off. Encourage them to develop their unique personalities and always treat them equally and fairly. To quell any worries, despite being interested in dollies, tea parties and dressing things up they are quite happy to play with Lego, pirates and mud as well. Most importantly, always know where the nearest toilet is!' Chris, father of three girls: Millie, Meredith and Nellie

Wisdom of Fathers

Dads do discipline

'You really do have to be consistent on the discipline front. My wife would be a lot softer with our son than I. She'd give him cuddles and tell me off for telling him off. I wasn't being over the top and when he got to two and really played up a lot we worked out that we needed to back each other up when telling him what he was doing wrong and not let him play us off against each other.' Paul, father of Louis at 30 months

'I take the view that my job is to produce an independent adult who is a good member of society – so in as far as is reasonable I treat Elias as an adult. He now (this is fairly recent) uses adult crockery and cutlery, he eats whatever we are eating, if he gets something out he puts it away. I actually really enjoy doing the adult things with him. So for example last weekend we went to a café to meet some friends. Elias was the only kid there. As we all had a hot drink – so did he. He sat in his high chair and has his own small hot chocolate with cream in a proper mug and drank it like an adult. And he joined in the conversation (... as far as possible). Seeing him enjoy and do those simple things is the thing I enjoy most.' Mike, father of Elias.

11 WORDS AND PICTURES

Child's Life: Weeks 41–44

WHAT'S HAPPENING WITH OUR BABY AT 11 MONTHS?

Waving goodbye, crawling and 'cruising' – all have featured as possible events in the last few chapter introductions but by now your youngster should be making some movements like this to communicate and just get around the house. Again they could be:

- Mastering the whole idea of 'dada' and 'mama' by this point and indicating what they want with gestures (see baby signing in Chapter 6).
- Developing an idea for the 'best use' of objects by now so will have sussed out that crayons are best for drawing, not so much for eating.
- Showing their bond with you and their mum through that stranger anxiety.
- Jabbering while you're in mid conversation with another adult or on the phone.

HOW CAN WE TAKE OUR BABY OUT FOR A HASSLE-FREE MEAL?

Eating out with your baby can be a challenging experience and you may well have taken on that challenge a lot earlier than now – but

THE NEW DAD'S SURVIVAL GUIDE

with your baby's first birthday looming this could be as good a time as ever to pass on some fatherly advice about taking your baby to a pub or restaurant to eat out. It's not so much about rules, as more a few pointers that parents need to consider beforehand.

- **Check kids can come:** Call ahead to see if the place you want to go to will cater for babies. Friends can recommend family-friendly places, while websites like www.childfriendly.co.uk have sections on pubs in popular UK destinations and holiday resorts that cater for kids too. If you're going somewhere new don't forget to reserve a high chair when you're booking a table.
- **Pick your moment:** Try to arrange meals out around your baby's routine to avoid any tiredness-induced tantrums at the table. It may help to order your kid's meal as soon as you're settled. You could walk them around or play with them to delay sitting at the table until their meal arrives.
- **Pack a plate:** While many family-friendly venues will stretch to a high chair and in some cases changing facilities in the toilets, don't expect any baby cutlery or plastic plates – if you're weaning your little 'un be sure to pack their own food plus a few extra spoons because some are sure to end up on the pub floor.
- **Let them feed themselves:** If you've been weaning them to feeding themselves at home, then let them do this – just check the plate and food isn't hot when it arrives.
- **Clear the table:** Make sure your baby can't reach out to grab any adult cutlery, glasses or bottles – and even if you do clear the area of them, keep a watch for sharp objects or hot plates being moved close to your baby during the service.
- **Have tricks up your sleeve:** Get into the habit of packing a toy, book or favourite cuddly plaything to keep your baby amused between making a mess with their food. An hour or so in a high chair surrounded by high-brow conversation can tire out a tot – get used to taking along some entertainment for them too.

- **Don't leave Baby behind:** As incredible as it sounds, some people, even the British Prime Minister, have had so much fun in the beer garden that they've left their little one behind.

Dad You Know?

Suck It and See

Don't worry so much about 'cleaning' a dropped dummy yourself. Research from the University of Memphis in 2013 revealed that the transfer of microbes which occurs when Dad or Mum suck on a dummy before popping it back into Baby's mouth can improve the bacterial diversity of babies' digestive systems and boost immunity.

Weird Things Babies Do

Head-banging

For some strange reason, just as babies develop the strength and awareness to sit and hold their heads upright some suddenly start doing 'head-banging' movements with similar gusto to the frenzied bit of 'Bohemian Rhapsody'. It's an understandably alarming sight, seeing your precious little gift of life rhythmically thwacking their cranium against the nursery furniture. This, along with a general 'rocking' habit, is sometimes seen as a sign of some kind of behavioural problem by parents but it's actually quite a common, comforting phase that around one in five babies go through – generally it's more likely in boys than girls.

Do mention it to the doctor or health visitor but DON'T try to reduce it by putting loose pillows in his or her cot as these have a much more dangerous suffocation risk. Do check that there are no sharp edges or loose screws in their cot that they could cut themselves on.

WHAT GAMES CAN I PLAY WITH OUR BABY NOW?

As their physical growth, intellectual development, dexterity and curiosity march on at a pace so there are more and more ways Dad and Baby can interact through play and keep building and cementing that bond. Okay it's still early doors for a game of FIFA 2014 on the Xbox admittedly, but there are plenty of activities you can do right now that'll be fun and have some hidden developmental plus points too:

Build and break

Creating little towers from blocks or stacks of soft toys helps build their dexterity, grip and lightness of touch – while smashing them down again gets them laughing and learning how things come together and apart. Stacking up plastic cups is another way to get them building, standing up and discovering 'toys' you hide inside cups too.

Hide and seek

When they're sat upright opposite you, play games that help develop their senses and curiosity. Hide their favourite – annoying – squeaking or rattling toy behind your back so that they try to seek it out. Use a noisy toy to give them audio clues and keep them alert as they wonder where their toy has gone.

Jolly jigsaws

Don't worry that they're not going to be following the picture on the box just yet – getting your son or daughter to share a puzzle with you isn't just a fun game to play, it'll sow the seeds of creating pictures and puzzles in their minds and help them work out how shapes fit together.

Splash down

Any watery bathtime games are going to be messy of course but they come with some hidden benefits too. Water fascinates babies – as dads who go to baby swim clubs will testify – and so will water games. Introduce them to the concept of pouring water into empty cups to fill them up – anything with funnels or spouts will add to the play and bring on their hand–eye co-ordination a treat.

More motion

With their upright body strength developing and their neck muscles firm enough to hold their head properly it's a good time for them to be pushed to and fro on the swings, to have little rides on the baby roundabout in the park or to start using one of those Cosy Coupe cars they drive with their feet.

Assault course

As they're finding their feet and getting used to cruising around the house using the furniture to stabilise themselves, dads can set them little courses to help develop their balance, co-ordination and walking skills. Place their toy at one end of the sofa, or line up a row of chairs, and encourage them to make their way along the route to get their prize. Give them a big cheer and a hug when they do.

KEEPING DAD 'APPY

While some mobile phone apps are useful during those first few months of fatherhood (see Chapter 2), others come into their own as your baby gets bigger and your needs change too. Stuart Dredge of Apps Playground is a dad who knows his apps – he reviews them for newspapers and devised appsplayground.com, a great website for children's apps reviews.

WOWDAD Maps

A must-have for dads out and about with their children, this provides listings for more than 13,000 baby-changing facilities, buggy-friendly restaurants, soft play areas and other venues.

https://itunes.apple.com/gb/app/wowdad-maps/id655533080?mt=8

Monsta Points

If you're working on your children's behaviour and want a digital alternative to the naughty step, this iPad reward chart app is well worth trying: it rewards kids for chores.

https://itunes.apple.com/gb/app/monsta-points-reward-system/id651049272?mt=8

Sesame Street Family Play

Coming up with a constant stream of ideas for games to play in the real world is hard. This app gives dads a helping hand, with more than 150 games sorted by location and number of children.

https://itunes.apple.com/gb/app/sesame-street-family-play/id690979001?mt=8

RockaBub

Zonked from sleep deprivation? Hope is in sight with this app from Australia, which offers a mixture of videos and text tips on dealing with sleep-challenged babies and toddlers.

https://itunes.apple.com/gb/app/rockabub-pro/id631060302?mt=8

23snaps

If Facebook isn't quite the thing to share your child's key life moments, 23snaps is well worth a look: a more private social networking app to share photos, videos and text with close friends and family.

https://itunes.apple.com/gb/app/23snaps-family-journal-private/id526481189?mt=8

HOW DO I READ TO MY BABY?

So you want to perfect your storytelling skills? Well, if you're sitting comfortably, then we'll begin ...

Research shows that when dads read to their babies and toddlers those kids usually grow up to do better at school than the ones who didn't get bedtime stories. With that in mind it's really a case of just making the time to tell them a tale, share a book with them and as they grow let them choose the books they'd like you to read.

It's because bedtime stories encourage speech and language development and help kids learn literacy skills that they're so important – but you get a double whammy because a book at bedtime also helps set in place healthy sleep patterns too.

Firstly, get into character ...

Bedtime stories should be told in a relaxed atmosphere (turn off the TV) and when possible with a bit of dramatisation on your part. Try reading in different voices or perform some of the actions in the story – the aim is to make the story more engaging and fun. (This will become more effective as your little boy or girl gets older but there's no harm in practising now.)

Have a regular read ...

As part of a bedtime routine your baby will love to hear your voice and will know that it's time to wind down ready for sleep. Don't feel that you need to have a different story every night at first, just get into the routine of reading and stick with the same book for as long as you can handle it! Hearing stories over and over again helps children become familiar with words and speech patterns too.

Moving to choosing ...

As your baby begins to respond to sounds, and becomes more engaged with objects and people for that matter, then look to choose bright and touchy-feely books with different textures and colours. Encourage your baby to touch the book as you read and talk about the pictures.

Also chooses books with rhymes and rhythm and some repetition – hearing rhyming words will help them later when they learn to read. Be prepared to say the words a little more slowly than you usually talk – this helps your baby hear the sounds you are making. Also try singing or reading rhymes to your baby with a bit of melody to soothe them and encourage their enjoyment of the book.

Read around ...

Don't be afraid to read out loud stuff you're reading – like the paper or from your iPad – when you're with your baby. Get them familiar with how reading works and let them see that it's important to you too. Also don't just stick to bedtime reading – bathtime reading books with tales like 'Five Little Ducks' are fun for your baby, and there's a good chance you'll end up reading it next time.

Reading up ...

As they get older get into a habit of asking open questions about the book to your child. It shouldn't be a test but it can help them build links between books and everyday life if you read a passage and ask questions like 'do you know any other cats who look like Six Dinner Sid?' Or 'what would you like to play on in the Shark In The Park's park?' Or 'this was due back to the library last year – do you think they accept credit card payments for fines?'

Great Books by Ages ...

Highly recommended books for babies and toddlers – from 0 to 2 – that dads like as well include:

The Very Hungry Caterpillar – Eric Carle

HUG – Jez Alborough

Where's Spot? – Eric Hill

We're Going on a Bear Hunt – Michael Rosen

Dear Zoo – Rod Campbell

Five Little Monkeys Jumping on the Bed – Eileen Christelow

Jungly Tails – an interactive fabric book from the Jelly Kitten range

That's Not My ... A series of books by Fiona Watt and Rachel Wells (Usborne) Touchy-feeling book – *That's Not My Bear* was a personal fave.

The 'Baby Touch' series of *Colours, Words* and *Numbers* books (Ladybird)

One Gorilla – Anthony Browne

Freight Train – Donald Crews

WHAT'S THE BEST WAY TO PHOTOGRAPH OUR BABY?

Photos of your son or daughter will be filling up picture frames around the house and postings on your social network site – mastering the art of taking great pics of your baby is therefore not only a useful one but could even spark a whole new money-making sideline. Babies aren't naturally inclined to sit still when you want them to – so if you're looking to take better baby pictures bear in mind the following:

- **Lighten up:** Great light can make a great photo – most studio shots will use a large soft light for baby photos.

Sometimes the sunlight through a net-curtained window will do the trick – or else sunlight reflected off of a light-coloured wall.

- **Prop up:** Toys and props are perfect for igniting a reaction from your baby – the one you're after is smiling and wide-eyed. Having someone just out of shot holding your baby's favourite cuddly bear could have the desired effect, but be quick with the snaps before your little one starts crying for their toy.
- **Eye up:** For attractive portraits take your shot from your kid's eye level or above to accentuate a baby's most endearing feature – its eyes. Keep the background simple, and, if you prefer, let them play with their toys and simply pick the best of a series of shots of them doing this.

What about passport photos?

To take your baby overseas you're going to need a passport – but getting a baby's passport photo taken is the kind of challenge that team-building weekends are made for.

The passport office do waive some of their look-like-a-convict picture restrictions for babies – their mouths can be smiling and babies eyes don't need to be solely focused forward to the camera.

However the photo does have to show your baby with its face against a plain, light background and he or she must be on their own – and facing forward. Prepare for some trial and error holding them upright – while you're out of shot – in a photo booth, without any toys or dummies appearing in the final picture either.

Some photo studio and even pharmacies can often do a decent job of this for not a huge fee by propping them against a white background and getting a series of shots for you to choose the best one from.

Dad You Know?

Parent Breaks

How long has it been since you and your partner went a whole day without talking about 'the baby'? When was the last time you and she spent some time together doing the kind of thing you loved doing before your son or daughter came along? Fair enough you may find that the time you get with your child is precious, and between sleeps and naps and your work pattern it may never be enough – but be sure not to neglect the relationship that bought that baby about in the first place. If you can't or don't want to get a babysitter but do want to get away for a few days look into groups like www.babygoes2.com – which lists hotels and resorts geared up especially for the needs of couples with young babies.

ANY TIPS FOR BUYING CLOTHES FOR OUR BABY?

The pace your child grows at will leave your mouth gaping and your wallet too. Be prepared to see your kid wear something only once before they've managed to grow out of it. Gifts of clothing at this age are a real bonus and there are plenty of nearly new websites and sales including those run by the NCT for parents to buy baby and toddler clothes from without break-ing the bank.

- If you're buying something for your baby remember to prepare for the growth spurts and 'upsize' the choice of clothing you go for.
- Look for easy-access clothes – with Velcro or poppers – because you're going to be changing them yourself for many more months.

- Draw around your kid's feet and get a template before you go shopping – it'll take some of the strain out of having to try on lots of pairs of shoes to find the right fit.

Dad You Know?

Fathers Go Farther

There's an assumption that parenthood brings with it stresses and strains that will drive you to an early grave. Wrong. In fact, the added life experience and exercise that comes with having little ones can do wonders for a man's heart. A 10-year study of 135,000 men carried out by researchers from Stanford University School of Medicine in California found that married men who have had no children are at a 17 per cent higher risk of cardiovascular-related (heart disease and stroke) death than those who have become fathers.

WHY THE BIG EMPHASIS ON TALKING TO A BABY?

Never miss an opportunity to encourage your baby to talk – basically by yacking away yourself to them at every opportunity. The more you do and the more words you use the faster they'll progress in their vocabulary and comprehension. Don't resort to 'baby talk' all the time either – they get plenty of 'coochie-coo'-like babble from the strangers they're introduced to every day. Let them get to know how you talk, the words you use, your tone and never shy away from joking with them.

According to a study presented to the Economic and Social Research Council's Festival of Social Science, dads who joke around pass on the tools for their children to think creatively, make friends and manage stress. So feel free to play court jester – your kids will thank you later.

Get the banter going with them as you change their nappy,

or feed or bathe them – and give them plenty of opportunity to chat back.

Keep the eye-to-eye contact strong and always try to help them make connections by holding up the nappy and saying 'nappy', or pointing to the cat and saying 'cat' or giving them 'choices' of food when they're eating.

Hold the slice of banana and the slice of carrot and say the names of each food as you offer it to them. They already have the picture of what they want to eat – you can provide the words and soon they'll be able to make choices and ask for exactly what they want.

Babies will develop their speech in their own time – don't be intimidated if your mate's kid can apparently recite the words to an Eminem track before they're walking while yours is still tongue-tied by 'daddy'. But the more you interact with them then sooner their speech will develop and the greater the grasp they'll have on new words. They will also be able to communicate their needs to you sooner and clearer – which will save you all a whole lot of tears. Other tried-and-tested ways to bring on the communication skills of a keen-to-learn baby and awkward-to-open-up-at-times-dad include:

Ditching the baby talk

Dads aren't comfortable with all that 'does Bubby want to play with ducky wucky' stuff. And who can blame them. It's not natural and many modern parenting experts will argue it's even detrimental to the child's conversation development. Go with what you feel happy with because as far as your baby's concerned right now it's the fact that you do talk to them that matters – not especially how you say it or what you say.

Get a feel for what they like

From a very early age babies nurture something of a preference for how they like to be spoken to. Some of them will react more to the loud voice or deeper tone of Dad while others instantly home in on what mum tells them and continue to respond devotedly to her requests even after they've left home. In order to make at least some kind of impression on your kid when they're in their teens, get in there now with plenty of chat from the start. Repetition is big with babies – especially in speech – though when it comes to watching *In The Night Garden* later down the line you'll see they love TV that repeats itself too.

Say it again, Dad

So with that love of repetition in mind don't baulk at re-reading the same nursery rhyme or singing the same little bedtime or bathtime song over and over again. Much like the now infamous 'routine', repetition provides wee bairns with a sense of comfort and security. Don't be afraid to mix it up a little – introducing funny little character voices to parts of some or dropping in words that are personal to them – but stick with the tried-and-tested repetition to provide them with some stability in this crazy new world they're discovering.

Easy on errors

As your baby learns to attach words to objects or make sounds that mirror yours they're going to trip up a little – verbally as well as physically – in the first few years. The temptation may be there for you or your partner to step in and correct every nuance for fear that you'll have to whisk them off to the speech therapists to correct the damage. In truth letting them express themselves and get confident in communicating is much more crucial at this stage than homing in on perfect, clipped newsreader English. Some of the funniest moments your baby will conjure up will come about from their own take on words as they learn to talk – cherish those 'hostipal' mispronunciations and keep a note of them!

Find phonics fun

Phonics is the way children are taught to read at school these days. It teaches them to decode the new written words they come across by sounding them out, or, in phonics terms, blending the sound-spelling patterns. Okay, it's a way off for you and your baby right now but the principles behind it help infants to structure words from the very start. It's as simple as saying the sounds of letters – 'Ah' for the letter 'A', 'buh' for B, etc., – as you point any out to them.

Weird Things Babies Do

Nosebleeds

Colds and a new-found habit of picking their nose can make nosebleeds a common condition in youngsters. If you're called upon to do the dad thing and save the day then sit your baby down and lean them slightly forward. Encourage them to breathe through the mouth and pinch the top of the nose for 5–10 minutes or until the bleeding stops – ensuring they continue to breathe okay through their mouth. If you're finding the bleeding isn't stopping or you're worried it may be caused by something more than just them having a good root around with their index finger, take them to a clinic.

Wisdom of Fathers

Mini-Me

'As he's got older our toddling son has helped with cleaning, cooking and even stripping wallpaper. I feel really strongly that babies/toddlers/children aren't a different species. They are independent people – they're just smaller, and they should be treated as such and act as such. This is of course as well as all the mad running round, building towers, watching CBeebies and eating mud.' Mike, father of Elias

IS IT A GOOD TIME TO HAVE ANOTHER KID?

Some couples will fall pregnant again within months of the birth of their first baby – others plan to do just that. As mad as it may seem – especially if the whole stress of the last pregnancy and birth is still as fresh in your memory as it is in your partner's – it's not unlikely that the pair of you may start discussing the possibility of trying for another baby around this time.

Think about it, there are plenty of plus points to having siblings with an age gap of 18–24 months beyond just the two-for-one deals on nappies. For starters, hand-me-down clothes will still be in vogue for the younger brother or sister! In reality, many couples decide to 'go for it' once they've got a taste for bringing up Baby – having children close in ages will, in theory, give each of them a like-minded playmate for years to come. They can share a bedroom for a few years before you need to look at finding a bigger home, and children get priority when it comes to many school places if they already have an older sibling already there.

Things to consider when talking about baby number two: firstly, talk to your GP about timing: some studies suggest you wait at least six months after the birth of your baby before trying for another. But every birth is different and your partner's own medical history will need to be considered – a gap of less than 17 months between babies has been linked with an increased risk of premature or underweight babies. But there are plenty of happy healthy families with siblings around a year apart. (The risks are highest for babies conceived less than six months after the birth of a previous child.)

Some practical matters: of course if you're really set on having another baby sooner rather than later then these practicalities aren't really going to have much sway on this. All the same, ask yourself:

- How's the current routine with your baby going now – what adjustments will you need to make during your wife/partner's pregnancy for your current baby and their childcare?

- Are you fit for it? Have the pair of you finally got back some semblance of energy and fulfilling night-time sleep – are you ready to disrupt all that again?
- Could you both cope with another baby coming between you – both physically and metaphorically?
- What are you both going to do about work? Is your partner prepared for being pregnant while working again and taking maternity leave again?
- How's the cash flow? You've already had a good glimpse at what it costs having another mouth to feed – so how will you get by with another baby? Can you tighten that belt further?

Your partner's age can have a much bigger influence on your chances of conceiving another child as a couple. If your partner has had her first child after the age of 30 – almost 350,000 children are born every year to women above the age of 30 in the UK – then the pair of you may need to talk to your GP at some point when it comes to trying for a second child.

There are no definite cut-off points as regards age and successful conception and pregnancy, but statistics show that fertility for women does begin to drop off from around the age of 30 onwards – with the decline becoming steeper after the age of 35. Mind you, in 2012 some 28,000 women in the UK became mothers above the age of 40.

According to the Royal College of Obstetricians 75 per cent of women aged 30 and 66 per cent of women aged 35 will conceive naturally and have a baby within a year of trying.

After this however it is increasingly difficult to fall pregnant – and statistically the chance of miscarriage rises too. Some women resort to fertility treatment, sometimes with multiple embryo implantations to improve their pregnancy success rate.

Your age could be a factor too. It's estimated that 8 in 10 couples who have sex regularly (every two or three days) without using any contraception will get pregnant within a year of trying. But a man's fertility levels can be affected by his age too – the older you are, the longer it may take you to get your partner pregnant. The chances of conception taking more than a year are judged to be around 8 per cent when you're under 25 – but by the time you're 35 that figure doubles.

WHAT ARE OUR OPTIONS IF WE'RE STRUGGLING TO HAVE ANOTHER BABY?

Around one in seven couples in the UK experience difficulty in conceiving (according to the Human Fertilisation and Embryology Authority). 'Secondary infertility' is the term used to describe the problems a woman may have conceiving a brother or sister for their first child. It's not uncommon – secondary infertility is actually more common than not being able to conceive at all in the first place – but it can come as a shock, especially if you conceived your first child quite easily. Modern fertility-assisting treatments can work wonders for many couples who want to have a baby – but there are many different types on offer.

To begin with, fertility experts will suggest you and your partner talk to your respective GPs who will be able to examine your background medical history and possibly suggest causes for infertility. Before you have to go down any medicalised route your GP may suggest that you or your partner make some lifestyle changes that could influence your fertility chances.

Alternately your partner could be prescribed medicine designed to stimulate her egg production.

It may be that you're advised to investigate further fertility treatments. One of the more commonly known is *in vitro* fertilisation (IVF). In IVF a woman's eggs are removed from the ovaries and fertilised with sperm in a laboratory dish before being placed in her womb.

Other versions of this include intracytoplasmic sperm injection (ICSI), which involves injecting a single sperm directly into an egg and the fertilised egg (embryo) is then transferred to the woman's womb. There are also intrauterine insemination (IUI) and gamete intrafallopian transfer (GIFT).

With IUI, the best-quality sperm are chosen before the treatment begins. With GIFT, the eggs are removed from the ovaries and the healthiest are selected and placed together with sperm in the woman's fallopian tubes.

For more information on treatments available to couples speak to your doctor and also check out the Infertility Network UK (www.infertilitynetworkuk.com).

HOW CAN I BOOST MY FERTILITY LEVELS?

When you do decide it's time to try for another baby you could improve the stock of your sperm with a few tried-and-tested tricks including:

Hang loose

Getting too hot around the testicles can slow down the rate of sperm production. A sack-full of research – including studies from the University of Milan – suggests that wearing looser underwear (boxers not briefs) and avoiding 'over-heating' behaviour like resting a lap-top on your lap could help improve your sperm activity. The National Fertility Association also recommends that men who work in hot conditions or drive for long periods each day avoid hot baths and instead spray their testicles with cool water.

Go nuts

Changing your diet to raise your zinc intake may have a beneficial effect on your sperm count too. Red meat, wholegrains, peanuts and dairy products are all good natural sources of zinc – some nutritionists or GPs may suggest using zinc supplements as a means of countering the harmful effects that pollution and chemicals on food can have upon the body's sperm production.

Ease off the booze

Having a first child could have driven you to drink, but if you're serious about having another baby and have concerns over your own fertility then quit the fags and cut down on the beer binges. Alcohol consumption has been linked to reduced levels of male hormones, like testosterone, and heighted levels of female ones, such as oestrogen, which may have a negative knock-on effect on your fertility capability.

Dad You Know?

Fear-therhood

'One in three new fathers report worries about financial pressures and fears about job stability.' Fatherhood Institute

WHAT ARE THE PROS AND CONS OF HAVING ANOTHER BABY SO SOON AFTER THE FIRST?

If your partner falls pregnant again and you're likely to have another baby so that the gap between the siblings will be two years or less, there are some major plus points to this.

- For starters you'll condense the time devoted to those initial, exhausting stages of parenthood. As a dad you won't have to go out shopping for many new baby accessories or go around baby-proofing the house again. You're armed and prepared for nappies, teething and night feeds – it's all fresh in the mind too.
- If you can both handle the concentration of demands on your time and resources then having babies so close to each other means that they will – in an ideal world – grow to soon be close siblings capable of sharing and enjoying similar activities.

- On the flip side of things, you're possibly going to be doubling the chaos that you've been through with your first child. As your first baby enters a challenging time of tantrums, near-constant activity and toilet training, so your partner and you will be devoting attention to a newborn baby too.
- Some parents describe it as being akin to 'crisis management' for the first couple of years at least – with relationships becoming strained and some complaining that they don't even have the time to enjoy their new roles as they lurch from the requirements of one needy nipper to another.

And as much as a new baby will eventually become an in-sync playmate for your first child, don't be surprised if there are some initial problems with the way the older one reacts to the arrival of their little brother or sister. Since your older child may barely have reached much older than one year old by the time the next one comes along they'll still be developing their own emotions and ways of communicating them. They could get confused and upset and not understand why. They may feel left out or even overwhelmed by what's being expected of them too. The advice of the experts is to make the older child an integral part of the care programme for their sibling – and be sure to give them the attention they desire too.

12 FATHER AHEAD

Child's Life: Weeks 45 and beyond

Take a moment to measure your baby and compare their stats with those at the start of your journey so far.

_____ weight at one year old.
_____ length from crown to toe.

WHAT'S HAPPENING WITH OUR BABY WHEN IT REACHES ONE YEAR OLD?

At this age your little boy or girl could well be doing all this and more:

- Expanding their vocabulary to more words ... like 'hello' and 'bye-bye' ... also 'woof' when they see a dog, or 'quack' when they see a pigeon ...
- They could start recognising their own reflection in a mirror and even staring at themselves intently as if they recognise that face from somewhere.
- They could be doing the words and gestures thing in unison – saying bye-bye and waving too.
- Picking up objects and trying to pick up and lift heavier things, like the cat if it's not careful.

- Drinking from a cup, feeding themselves with a spoon and picking up food with their fingers to eat.
- Standing upright unaided and toddling around without 'crashing' too often.
- Not only could they be playing games such as peekaboo, but some babies around this time will start mimic actions such as talking on a telephone or sweeping up.
- Some will start to get to grips with putting objects inside objects and working out 'puzzles' such as which lid fits on which container.
- They may even know basic body parts and can point to them when asked – good with 'head' or 'tummy', not so good with 'olfactory canal'.
- Your baby could by this time be developing a preferred handedness – more inclined to take objects in their right or left hand. And throw them at you.

WHAT'S THE ROUTINE NOW THEY'RE A YEAR OLD?

Your baby will still be napping and feeding in the little-and-often way that the health experts say us adults should too. At around 12 months their routine will probably feature a midday nap only – with a lot more solids than before but similar bedtime routine.

FIRST BIRTHDAY

HOW DO DADS DO FIRST-BIRTHDAY PARTIES?

Ideally your kid's first birthday is a landmark not to be missed. Not only is this a momentous occasion for your child – though they'll be pretty clueless as to what's going on – but it's one hell of a gig for you and your child's mum too. The pair of you have experienced 12 months of full-on parenthood. Undoubtedly challenging at times and memorable in many ways – you certainly deserve a celebratory treat too.

But first, a few pointers for dads playing a part in organising that first birthday:

- **Networking:** Okay, it seems a little early to be setting up some social event in order to tap up good contacts, but your baby's first-birthday party could have its networking uses too. Inviting lots of other babies – and of course their parents – enables you to compare and contrast and swap useful tips.
- **Event planning:** This is first of what may well be a long line of parties you could be hosting – and others that you'll be attending. When your child gets older there'll be other factors such as child entertainers, trips to the play centre or possibly more creative 'parties' such as making their own pottery or pizzas. But for now it's pretty simple – and a lot less expensive. Invite some friends and their babies around – provide food for the adults, party snacks for older siblings and leave the other one year olds to their parents' own devices.
- **Time it right:** Aim to dovetail the party in with your child's routine, so that they won't get ratty or need a nap just when you're planning to wheel out the birthday cake.
- **Take time out:** Make your baby's first-birthday party a special occasion, even if it's just you as a family that are celebrating it by taking the day off work. Get into the habit of breaking off from the nine-to-five and switching off the work phone for events like this one.
- **Have presents:** Friends may bring a little gift for your baby and you could make one of your own for your baby. Okay, buy one if you're not especially skilful at creating wonderful toys from wood or the like, but do turn your creative capabilities to recording the event.
- **Create a first-birthday film:** Take some film footage of your baby on their first birthday, maybe being given their presents or staring with a look of quizzical fear at the

candle stuck in the top of their birthday cake. A great gift, which they may not appreciate now, but will have rewards in years to come, would be to put together a first-year photo album. Use it to keep some 'landmark' photos – first steps, trips out, etc., – that have happened over the past 12 months along with any little mementoes.

WHAT THE HELL ARE PARTY BAGS?

Oh yes ... the party bag. If you've not done kid's parties before then this is an essential element – especially as your child gets older. It's a gift for all the friends that will be coming to the party by way of a thank you. It's unlikely that party bags will be handed out at a first birthday party ... but don't be shocked if they are. With older kids it's usually a collection of sweets and maybe a small toy for them to take away. Most kids aren't too discerning as to what they'll get in the bag – but parents can be. In the competitive world of parenting some children may be blackballed from attending a friends party if the quality of the gifts handed out at their party wasn't up to scratch.

WHAT MAKES A GREAT TOY FOR A ONE-YEAR-OLD BABY?

As your son or daughter becomes more dexterous and mobile so you'll find that their playthings may need to become more challenging or more engaging. Use their first birthday as a good excuse to have a rummage through the toy box. If you're making a birthday list for them, consider including some of these on there:

Push-along toys

A little kart with a pushchair-like handle – some of these double up as a storage container and a sit-on-and-ride toy too. Some of these may be quite familiar – there's a Thomas The Tank Engine one that's especially popular with toddling boys. These are great for bringing on your baby's walking and balance skills. They can stand up and push this around – using it as a support in the process too. They can load and unload it – always a popular pastime with one year olds and perfect for improving their dexterity.

Puzzles and shapes

Keep on buying your baby toys or puzzles that require them to sort things into order or to fit one shape into another. Along with helping them to solve simple problems and continue to develop their motor skills, these games are also a lot of fun and something the pair of you can play. Handing each other blocks to fit into the correct slot encourages your baby to share and play with others.

Activity centres

Moving on from that play mat they may have had in the first few months, this toy also has a range of activities – though much more advanced than simple dangling mobiles. Babies can press buttons, sort shapes, ring bells – some activity centres even come with 'grown up' accessories like a phone or mini calculator. Toys like this provide your baby with an instant response to their action – they learn that their involvement results in a bell ringing or a buzzer going off. They're able to fulfil that main purpose – for your little 'un to enjoy themselves – and are also something babies can play with on their own.

Bouncing balls

Balls take on a whole new ball game when your baby is able to stand up and start bouncing them for himself. Chasing them around the house also helps in their walking development.

Bucket and spade

Toddlers have a thing for filling things up – and tipping things back out again, so a bucket and spade should be packed in the storage section of the buggy whenever you're off to the park. If they're playing in the sand-pit or you're just digging around in the garden it's an ideal toy for them to join in with.

Click bricks

The next step after building blocks are plastic bricks that interlock. Duplo is a baby version of Lego, designed not to be swallowed. Babies can bind the chunky, colourful blocks together to build towers or stack up as they go from sitting to standing.

Activity books

Pop-up books and ones with pull-out tabs to make characters move encourage children to take a further interest in books. You can also get simple story books at this age which come with a selection of textures they can enjoy getting a feel for.

Dad You Know?

Dads Make Great Playmates

The rough and tumble play that dads and their kids often engage in is, according to research, a vital part of a child's development. A 2012 study from the Fathers and Families Research Program at the University of Newcastle in Australia, highlighted how the horseplay that fathers and their young children do helps shape the child's brain and even builds their self-confidence and concentration. 'This is a key developmental stage for children in that preschool area between the ages of about two-and-a-half and five,' explained Richard Fletcher, the lead researcher.

NEXT STEPS

SHOULD I LOOK AT UPSIZING TO A BIGGER BUGGY?

That buggy or travel system you bought back before baby was born or just after may have seen some action these past 12 months.

Don't be surprised if it needs a bit of a clean-up at least – or even an overhaul. Just check the screws and clips are all in place and the wheels are still tightly secured to the axle – in short, give it a service. As your baby gets bigger or the seasons change you may want to shift to a lighter, more manoeuvrable model – or more likely your partner will want to and you'll possibly be part of the consultation process.

If you're after an upgrade – or just want a spare for hulking away on holiday with you – look at trade-in websites like: www.pushchairtrader.co.uk which can flag up offers in your area if you tap in your postcode.

WHY DOES OUR BABY NEED EVEN MORE JABS?

Your baby's immune system has come on leaps and bounds since their birth and they are much more resilient now. (Your own health on the other hand may well have deteriorated over this period, with you showing stark symptoms of 'knackered'.) But they will still need another health review and another round of vaccinations at around the one-year mark including:

Check-up

This is usually from the health visitor – with a focus on language and learning. They may also help with issues such as diet and even behaviour. You may feel like this is a bit of an intrusion but it can be a useful chance for you and your partner to raise any concerns you may have and to take on some tips that you'll need to prepare for your child becoming a toddler.

Within a month of your child's first birthday they will be given their next set of vaccinations:

MMR *(measles, mumps and rubella)*

This gives your child a taster of these illnesses in order that their body's defences can deal with them should they even come into contact with them (which they may well do when they start mixing with other kids). The NHS advice is to get your baby inoculated and ensure they have the follow-up jabs.

Hib/Men C

A two-in-one injection for your baby that boosts their protection against the potentially fatal meningitis C and potentially high scoring Scrabble ailment: Haemophilus influenzae type b (Hib). The Hib/Men C is a booster vaccination given to all babies in the UK shortly after their first birthday (as part of the NHS childhood vaccination programme) and follows on from the Hib jab they would have had as part of the 5-in-1 vaccine at 8, 12 and 16 weeks old. (They should also have had the Men C vaccine at 12 and 16 weeks too.)

PCV

The pneumococcal vaccination (pneumo jab) protects against a bacterial infection that can lead to septicaemia (blood poisoning) and meningitis. It's a bug that can affect anyone, though children under the age of two are at a higher risk of complications should they get it. The PCV jab is given to babies as part of the same NHS programme.

IS IT OKAY FOR OUR BABY TO STILL BE BREASTFEEDING BEYOND YEAR ONE?

If your partner is happily maintaining breastfeeding at this stage your baby won't just still be benefitting from nourishment as nature intended. Along with a hearty dose of growing calories there are of course vitamins, enzymes and immunity boosters in the mix too. Research suggests that toddlers who are breastfed are statistically less likely to get ill too.

It can be even tougher for your partner though, as a stigma continues to exist surrounding breastfeeding of older babies. She may feel pressured to wean your baby solely on to solids before she really wants to – or else she may be given unfounded advice such as 'breastfeeding beyond 12 months makes a kid overly dependent.'

If she's still enjoying breastfeeding then your role as a dad and partner should be to actively encourage and support her, so long as it's what she want to do. Some dads may feel awkward about the process from the very start, but talking about how you and she feel about it, why she wants to continue with it and learning about the many long-term benefits for your baby will help you come to terms with what's really just another novel experience to put on that list.

WHAT KINDS OF SOLID FOOD SHOULD OUR BABY BE EATING TOO?

With your child now chomping their way through the weaned regime and stuffing solids in their gob at a rate of knots, it's worth checking that you're not only giving them interesting new tastes and flavours to try but that you're also ticking the nutritional intake box and ensuring that they're getting all the right foods for a growing baby's diet.

It may seem like foods fall into two categories – those that end up in the mouth or on the floor – but there are those crucial five-a-day food groups that you need to ensure your nipper is getting access to.

Fruit and veg

These are one of the easier, nutritious and baby-friendly groups. They're easy to cut and store. They're cheap and they're not at all fattening or harmful (so long as you peel them and watch your baby as they're eating pieces of course). Fruit and veg are essential for adding fibre to your baby's diet too – which in turn will keep their digestive system and bowels ticking over ... much to the delight of the nappy changer.

Milk and dairy

These provide calcium for bones and teeth of course – they're also useful for protein at this age too. However, a baby's immune system can react to the proteins in cow's milk and spark an allergy that's common in around seven per cent of infants. Babies with eczema are also at a higher risk of having a milk allergy. (That's not the same as a lactose intolerance, which is much rarer.)

Bread, cereals and potatoes

Starchy carbs may not sound too easy on a teething tot's mouth – until you consider that pasta and rice also fall into this category. Great for energy among other things, pasta jars and baby rice provide an ideal stepping stone from breasts or bottles to solid dishes. They're not the worst baby meals for dads to tuck into either.

Fats and oils

It's essential that you go against all adult diet instincts and marketing and go for full-fat foods when feeding your baby. Making dairy products and even fish dishes part of your little one's meal plan will raise their intake of the kinds of vitamins that keep their bones, skin and organs growing well.

Meat and fish

These overlap with the fats and oils of course – but there's also the issue here on whether you're raising your baby to eat meat or not. Vegetarian babies are not different in their health and development to meat-eating ones – provided both are getting a balanced diet and not being stuffed with masses of processed food and empty-calorie, high-sugar sweets and snacks of course.

If you're a man who's keeping close tabs on his own dietary intake in a bid to stay healthy and keep in shape, you may want to ensure your son or daughter's diet follows similar lines too. This doesn't mean pumping them with Maximuscle shakes after a gruelling session playing with the Tomy activity centre, but you can dig deeper into good food for babies by reading the smart nutrition for toddlers and babies section at websites like www.smanutrition.co.uk – or booking time with the local health visitor or clinic.

WALKING

WHEN WILL OUR BABY START WALKING ALL THE TIME?

Even at 14 months many toddlers are still toying with a mix of standing, shuffling, crawling and squatting down again. Walking backwards may be a new trick among the more experienced walkers at this age.

How can I help with their walking?

Useful stuff dads can do to help bring on their child's walking includes getting hold of one of those push-along toys that encourage them to get upright and shuffle around the house with them. These 'toddle toys' are great for your baby to learn to walk independently but just make sure they're stable and don't topple backwards too easily. The ones that double as a truck or toy carrier often have a wide base and work best.

Just holding out your arms and encouraging them to walk towards you – extending the distance every time – is a whole lot simpler and less expensive.

Climbing over the furniture can be actively encouraged as it helps your baby to become more proficient in their co-ordination – as should attempting a few stairs, under your close supervision. By around 18 months he or she could well find going up stairs a doddle but may still need a hand going down them.

However, 'baby walkers' – toys that your baby sits in and propels themselves forward – are discouraged by a lot of groups in the UK, including RoSPA, and the USA because of accidents linked to their use. The Chartered Society of Physiotherapy (CSP) has even called for a ban on baby walkers – they're outlawed in Canada too – as physiotherapists blame them for 4,000 injuries per year and also claim that baby walkers 'disrupt the ability of children to develop walking and visual skills and stop them from properly exploring their surroundings.' It's also the line from the American Academy of Pediatrics that babies get a bit lazy with walkers and their upper leg muscles may not develop correctly.

POTTY TRAINING

HOW MUCH LONGER WILL OUR BABY NEED NAPPIES FOR?

As much as you may want to, you can't fast track your baby into toilet training. They're a few months away from that if you're reading this chapter in sync with their first year – but if you're glancing at this when your tot's around 24 months old, then, dear Father, you could be able to 'muck in' with their shift from pooing in a nappy to pooing in a potty. To prime your wee one for this you need to:

Shop for a potty

Get them into the habit of sitting on a new, broad-based potty. There are plenty of fun character ones available, some of which even come with accompanying 'bog-side' reading material to making doing a dump doubly fun.

Ease them in

Never force them to sit on it, just try explaining to them what it's for and – at regular times like just before bathtime – let them try it out for size. If they produce any goods when they're sat on it be sure to heap them with plenty of 'well done' praise. (While you're gagging.) Encourage them to do it, just avoid making it something you post on Facebook though.

Sit and whistle

'Toddlers take their time about making this process a habit,' suggests Dr Maggie Renshaw, a child psychologist and advisor to nappy giants Pampers.com. Don't be surprised if your kid continues switching between potty and toilet, with nappy and some bed-wetting thrown in for a year or two. 'When they're able to start telling you that they've done a poo or wee – or even better that they feel the need to, that's an ideal time to get them to the potty,' suggests Renshaw.

Look for signs

You may even spot the signs that they're about to go – standing still or reddening of their face or concentrated look on their face while half-staring into space. Once they're familiar with the potty make a point of asking them if they need to go – you may notice that they get into a regular time habit. Don't nag them or make them anxious about using the toilet or not going when they should. 'Once they're used to going you'll still need nappies for them at night – they will probably still have a few accidents,' says Renshaw.

Wisdom of Fathers

Potty time

'We had a few problems at first getting Abi to use a potty. We let her choose one from the shop herself – but when my wife or I plonked her on it she started kicking off. We thought she wasn't ever going to get it and then when we stayed at my sister's she saw her cousin using a potty. He's about the same age as her – I don't know if it was his influence for sure, but soon after that we found her sat on it in the loo. She's been using it and the toilet ever since.'
Chester, father of Abi

WHAT LIES AHEAD?

Your first year of fatherhood will have changed you for sure and ideally have prepared you for some of the challenges you're going to face going forward. Some of the skills you've learnt in communicating, comforting and bonding with your baby already will serve you well as the joys of walking, talking, potty training and the 'terrible twos' take hold. The foundations you've set in place for safety, discipline, diet and child development will be tailored as your baby grows and as you learn more about them.

The work you've done in re-shaping your lifestyle, your home, your work patterns, your social life and, most of all, your relationship with your partner will no doubt undergo many more changes because as you've no doubt realised there's always, always your child to think of before you make so many decisions these days.

Make time for yourself and your partner to celebrate your baby's first year together too. It's a great time for the pair of you to congratulate yourselves for the success you've made of doing something that probably terrified you both at first. Take a moment to think about your confidence in the role and how, a year or so ago, you'd never done the vast array of skills you've now mastered with your baby – such as feeding, changing, bathing, dressing and feeding again.

Once your baby is up and running it really does become a whole new ball game. Their independence, inquisitiveness and physical and mental progress will literally keep you on your toes for years to come. There's so much you can do to continue playing your part and influencing their development as they build up towards starting school full-time that it easily merits an entire book of its own. If you have the energy you may want to consider writing it too? Well done, Dad, and good luck for the future ...

Wisdom of Fathers

Celebrating Your Role

'The three most enjoyable things about being a new dad right now would be – firstly – his smiles, especially first thing in the morning. They break my heart every time he does them. Secondly is seeing him grow, developing on a day-by-day basis – he's making more and more noises and trying to grab things and supporting himself on his legs. Thirdly, I really enjoy bathtime with him too, probably as that is really our time together and it feels really special.' Steve, father of Logan

NEW DADS ...
ACCORDING TO NEW MUMS

Before I pass on a few useful contact details – here's what new mums told me their husbands and boyfriends did after the baby was born, to make themselves a saint or sinner. Thanks to Mumsnet.com for permitting to me to carry out this impromptu survey.

Codes:
DH = Darling Husband
DD = Darling Daughter
DS = Darling Son

What's the best and worst thing your husband/partner did in the first year of fatherhood?

Best thing: When DD was a newborn DH changed her nappy after I'd fed her so that I didn't have to get out of bed at night.

Worst thing: Inviting friends and family to the hospital to meet the baby when I was recovering from the birth, was trying to establish breastfeeding and definitely wasn't up for visitors.

Best thing: DH spent the first night in a different room with our son asleep on his chest – just bringing him in for feeds so I could catch up on a little sleep and recover from the birth.

Worst thing: DH let his boss bully him into returning to work after just five days of paternity leave with our second child. Two days later our eldest got chickenpox. That was tough.

Best thing: He co-slept with DS through choice many times without needing to be nagged/encouraged. Quite the opposite, in fact. Also cuddled DS topless, frequently, after me telling him about skin-to-skin helping bonding – the boy is 19 months and an utter daddy's boy.

Worst thing: Probably the move to England when DS was 16 days old and having to put up with my in-laws moaning and sniping regularly.

Best thing: Everything! DH fed me with everything I loved, waited on me hand and foot, made sure I had absolutely nothing to do but breastfeed and sleep. And he bought me very nice jewellery!

Worst thing: I'd gone to hospital with no time to spare so had no bag, clothes or crucially, underwear. After my speedy birth, I asked him to bring me some underwear. He turned up having rooted through my drawers with the most diaphanous, tiny, delicate scraps of lace he could find – both bra and knickers. Last worn on my honeymoon, I think.

Best thing: He cleaned the house from top to bottom and did all the laundry while me and DS were in hospital so I had nothing but DS to think about when we got home.

Worst thing: When I was tired/stressed he would whisk DS off to his mum's to 'give me a break' – the thought was there but it wasn't really the answer.

Best thing: Amazing cheerleader all through breastfeeding and supported me no matter what I chose to do.

Worst thing: Struggled to understand why I wanted quiet time at home, not a night out getting drunk.

Best thing: Bought amazing food to the hospital, did everything after I came home (C-section), really supported me with breast-feeding and not wanting visitors.

Worst thing: After going overnight fishing when baby was three weeks old, going straight to bed telling me I had no idea how tired he was!

Best thing: Put up with my relatives visiting, and cooked and looked after them all.

Worst thing: Exclaimed what a quiet night it had been – after I had breastfed baby THREE times in the night!

Best thing: Always supporting me with breastfeeding, reading the benefits, boosting confidence, speaking to friends' wives and passing on info.

Worst thing: Nothing, he was amazing. Does loads of house-work, supports my career, is an egalitarian, selfless man.

Best thing: Completely waited on me hand and foot, even slept in the other room with DD when she was tiny with expressed milk on hand so I could have a full night's sleep at least once a week, even though he worked full time.

Worst thing: Trip to London to stay at his mum's when DD was only a couple of weeks old and I was still exhausted, sore and struggling to breastfeed. I cried in the night and he told me I should have just said no, when during planning it clearly wasn't an option.

USEFUL RESOURCES

Where possible I've included contact details or website links to organisations that you may want or need to contact during the first year or so of your child's life within the pages of the relevant topic. Just as the role and the involvement of the father in child-rearing has changed so much over the past couple of generations so the support groups for, the advice given to and the opinions of new fathers have evolved too. I hope that by you contributing your own experiences to me via NewDadsTalk@twitter.com you'll be able to pass on your own useful advice to the next generation of men in your shoes.

Only Dads

Advice and support for single parents on financial issues, debt, legal problems and health and relationships, among other topics. www.onlydads.org

Fathers Reaching Out

Support group for partner of sufferers from postnatal depression. www.fathersreachingout.com

British Association for Counselling and Psychotherapy

Register of qualified counsellors available to assist new parents. www.bacp.co.uk

Dad.info

Useful website featuring news and advice for fathers. Dad.info is responsible for the advice cards for new fathers that are distributed through maternity wards around the UK. The website features legal and work-related tips too.
www.dad.info

Fatherhood Institute

The UK's fatherhood think-tank, the institute is responsible for collating research on fatherhood-related issues, influencing public debate on fathers and their role in society as well as promoting training and support services and helping to shape government family policy.
www.fatherhoodinstitute.org

Gingerbread

Parenting advice and support option info for single-parent families.
www.gingerbread.org.uk

Family Lives

This charity runs a 24/7 support line for new parents 0808 800 2222.
www.familylives.org.uk

Family Rights Group

A charity that advises families whose children are involved with or need children's services because of welfare needs or concerns.
www.frg.org.uk

The NCT (National Childbirth Trust)

Find your local NCT antenatal classes including standard and specialised groups run by this independent charity.
www.nct.org.uk

NHS parent craft classes

Available through the maternity services department of your chosen hospital. For more info contact:
www.nhs.uk/Planners/pregnancycareplanner

The Red Cross First Aid for Babies classes

Provides courses designed to teach a range of first-aid skills to cope with emergency situations for babies and children.
www.redcrossfirstaidtraining.co.uk

St John Ambulance

Run courses for new parents on emergency procedure in the event of your baby becoming ill or suffering an accident.
www.sja.org.uk

Cleft Lip and Palate Association

Specialist information website on treatment procedures in relation to this birth defect.
www.clapa.com

The Lullaby Trust

Charity researching the causes of cot death with advice and information for new and expectant parents on reducing the risk.
www.lullabytrust.org.uk

Boots Parenting Club

Free online parenting tips and advice and offers for useful baby stuff – including regular email tips and links for new dads.
www.boots.com

Down's Syndrome Association

Promoting awareness of the issues surrounding Down's syndrome, improving knowledge of the condition and championing the rights of those with it.
www.downs-syndrome.org.uk

British Infertility Counselling Association

Resource site for counsellors and those seeking information on infertility problems.
www.bica.net

The Men's Health forum

Expert-backed advice on problems conceiving and issues such as erectile dysfunction can be sourced via their website:
www.malehealth.co.uk

NHS Choices

Provides insight into what steps to take if you're having trouble conceiving.
www.nhs.uk/Conditions/Infertility

The Family Planning Association

Contraception advice and information on options available to new parents.
www.fpa.org.uk

NHS Smokefree

NHS free advice line and website with information on smoking cessations service and nicotine replacement products. 0800 022 4332
http://smokefree.nhs.uk

Twins and Multiple Births Association (TAMBA)

One-stop resource for those expecting more than one baby. Set up by parents of twins, triplets and higher multiples and interested professionals, it's the only UK-wide organisation that directly helps tens of thousands of parents meet the unique challenges that multiple birth families face.
www.tamba.org.uk

Also see The Multiple Births Foundation, Queen Charlotte's & Chelsea Hospital, 0208 383 3519.
www.multiplebirths.org.uk.

Working Tax Credits and benefits

The government do provide advice for working parents rights via www.gov.uk/child-tax-credit and information on all forms of financial childcare support at www.gov.uk/child-benefit. Information on benefits you may be entitled to can also be found via www.hmrc.gov.uk/childbenefit/.

Baby gear

Events like The Baby Show (www.thebabyshow.co.uk) are great places for comparing the wide world of baby gear in just the one long trudge.

The NCT (www.nct.org) run nearly new sales for everything from buggies to baby feeding bottles around the UK.

Car seats can be found at Mothercare and Halford, plus online at the manufacturers websites such as Britax, www.britax.co.uk, and Maxi-Cosi, www.maxi-cosi.co.uk. Check out the website for your car manufacturer too and see what they recommend.

Pushchairs can also be sourced via the individual brand websites – e.g. Bugaboo, www.bugaboo.com, or Maclaren, www.maclarenbaby.com

Alternately try the high street store such as Mothercare (www.mothercare.com)

To find your nearest re-useable nappy cleaning service contact the National Association of Nappy Services (NANS) – www.changeanappy.co.uk – or your local NCT to find out about laundry services.

ACKNOWLEDGEMENTS

Thanks to all the experts and parents who've provided explanations, advice, tips and testimony towards the writing of this book. In no particular order of merit thanks to: Jane Keogh, first-aid specialist with the British Red Cross; Jonathan Lewis of Balance Physiotherapy; Sheila Merrill, head of home safety at RoSPA; Dr Abigail Locke; Dr Maggie Renshaw; Dr Jenny Sutcliffe; Sally Randle, Independent Midwives (IMUK); Clare Byam-Cook; Siski Green; Little Dippers; Working Families; Denise Knowles at Relate; Mark Williams of Fathers Reaching Out; Rob Spedding; Tom Harrow of Findababysitter.com; and Jay Blades of Men Behaving Dadly. Also thanks to Edith Garrard at British Airways, Peter Walker at Baby Massage, Nick Coffer and Mike Jones.

To the fathers who've provided insight into their journeys – thank you. That's Adam, Andy, Paul, Paul S., Dominic, Michael, Sunil, Steve, Keiran, Kevin, Richard, Patrick, Conan, Rob, Allan, Dan, Sam, Chris, Lee, Tom and Chester.

Thanks to Kate Latham for her diligent editing and helpful feedback. Thanks to Stuart Dredge of Apps Playground.

A big thank you also to Susanna Abbott and Catherine Knight at Vermilion for their feedback and encouragement – and to Patrick Walsh at Conville & Walsh.

BIBLIOGRAPHY AND FURTHER READING ...

Berkmann, Marcus: *Fatherhood: The Truth* (Vermilion, 2005)

Biddulph, Steve and Shaaron: *The Complete Secrets of Happy Children* (HarperCollins, 2003)

Brott, Armin: *The New Father* (Mitchell Beazley, 2005)

Burgess, Adrienne: *Fatherhood Reclaimed: The Making of the Modern Father* (Vermilion, 1998)

Burrows, Gideon: *Men Can Do It!* (NGO Media, 2013)

Crider, Michael: *The Guy's Guide to Surviving Pregnancy, Childbirth and the First Year of Fatherhood* (Da Capo Press Inc., 2005)

Duerden, Nick: *The Reluctant Fathers' Club* (Short Books, 2009)

Giles, Stephen: *From Lad to Dad* (White Ladder Press, 2008)

Hallows, Richard: *Full Time Father: How to Succeed as a Stay at Home Dad* (White Ladder Press, 2004)

Lamb, Michael E.: *The Role of the Father in Child Development* (John Wiley & Sons, 2010)

Moussaieff Masson, Jeffrey: *The Evolution of Fatherhood* (Ballantine Books Inc, 2004)

Nichols, Powell, Lanier and Egerton: *Dadlabs Guide to Fatherhood* (Quirk Books, 2009)

Rapley, Gill and Murkett, Tracey: *Baby-Led Weaning: Helping Your Baby to Love Good Food* (Vermilion, 2008)

Russell, Dr Graeme & White, Tony: *First-Time Father* (Finch Publishing, 2007)

INDEX